"...
whose p
—Henry David Thoreau

"I don't care too much for money.
Money can't buy me love."
—John Lennon, Paul McCartney

"A loaf of bread, a jug of wine and thou . . ."
—The Rubáiyat of Omar Khayyám

"Let that which is wanting in income
be supplied by frugality."
—Alfred Henderson

"A penny saved is a penny earned."
—Ben Franklin

"Men do not realize
how great a revenue frugality is."
—Cicero

"Resolve not to be poor:
whatever you have, spend less."
—Samuel Johnson

To my father.
For his creativity and energy,
but especially for his "cheap" genes.

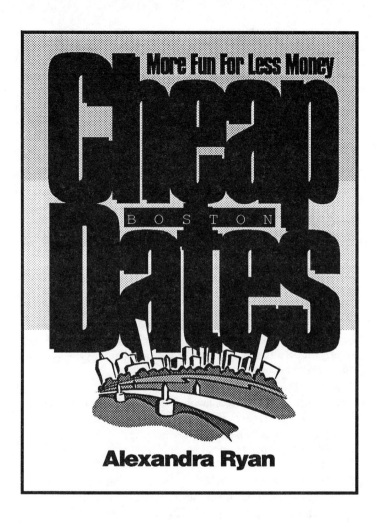

More Fun For Less Money

Cheap Dates

BOSTON

Alexandra Ryan

World Leisure Corporation
Hampstead, NH • Boston, MA

HELP UƩ FIND MORE CHEAP DATEƩ

If you have a Boston CHEAP DATE you would like to share
with others, send in your suggestion for possible inclusion
in the next edition of this guide.
Send all CHEAP DATE suggestions to:

World Leisure Corporation
Cheap Dates
P.O. Box 160
Hampstead, NH 03841

Copyright © 1996 by Alexandra Ryan

Cover design by Concialdi Design, Frankfort, IL.

Back cover photograph by Karen Cummings

Illustrations by Len Shalansky, Warwick, RI; (401) 738-3215

Cheap Dates™ is a trademark of World Leisure Corporation

Distributed to the trade in USA by
LPC Group, Login Trade Division, 1436 West Randolph Street,
Chicago, IL 60607; (312) 733-8228, (800) 626-4330.

Distributed to the trade in Canada by
E.A. Milley Enterprises, Inc., Locust Hill,
Ontario L0H 1J0, Canada, tel. (800) 399-6858.

Distributed to the trade in U.K. by Roger Lascelles,
47 York Road, Brentford, Middlesex TW8 0QP Tel. 0181-847 0935.

Mail Order, Catalog and Special Sales by
World Leisure Corporation, 177 Paris Street, Boston, MA 02128.
Tel: (617) 569-1966, fax: (617) 561-7654,
e-mail: wleisure@aol.com

ISBN: 0-915009-46-3

THANKS

To use "cheap" pejoratively — just once — it would be cheap of me not to acknowledge the many people who made suggestions, went on dates, and worked hard on this book.

To my mother, a dutiful fact checker and
also contributing to the "cheap" gene pool.
A special thanks to Peter Fivel for finding Charlie and for
being the best date a girl could have.
To Charlie Leocha for sharing a love of cheap things and for
being willing to publish a book about it.
To Jim Thompson: I *have* learned the difference
between "your" and "you're!"

To the girls of Winston Flowers: Parnel Ley, Deanna Joseph,
Ellen Harrel (thanks for the photos!), Anne Sovie, Nina
Samoiloff, Cathy Somers and to Alex Winston—thanks for your
help and ideas. And for their special inputs: thanks to Peter
Martin, Frank Ledogar, Tom Keller, Douglas O'Reilly, Paul
Noonan, Megan Lewis (and her car), Eve Kaplan, Hania Khuri
and Annie Jessup (enjoy your dinner in Canada!).
Thank you to Michael Mungavin at MotoPhoto.
And to all the other dates who didn't get mentioned.

A very special thanks to Todd Vincent for his encouragement
from the beginning, for his wonderful creativity,
and for being a dear friend.

CONTENTS

Cheap Dates
Boston

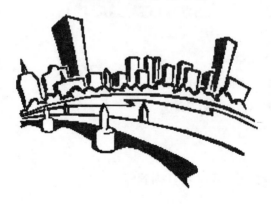

INTRODUCTION

People are obsessed with dating. Especially young people. Dating is the gateway to romance, and romance is in. But then, romance was never out. Through the centuries, romance has been the most consistent theme of poems, plays and stories. Your love life determines your well-being far more than a job, a grade or a car does, or ever could.

One of the most important and enjoyable pursuits of life is the search for a lifelong mate. Finding this mate is often a long, drawn-out process, taking years of trial and error. This is not to say that the process of searching for that certain someone cannot be wonderfully exciting; but before you find the one right person, there are bound to be a glut of dates with the wrong ones.

So it comes down to dating—and lots of it. It is supposed to be a fun exploration that is exciting and educational, but somewhere along the way dating acquired a bad name. All too often it leads to a dull waste of time and with little gained except maybe a painfully funny story to tell your friends.

Besides having lost much of its sparkle, dating has grown far too expensive. Having a social life has become a real wallet killer:

it's truly a wonder that we don't all reach the altar with empty pockets and a mate we hardly know. Dating needs to be jazzed up and priced down.

This is where *CHEAP DATES* steps in.

I was born of Cheap Date genes. My father was the ultimate Cheap Dater: a struggling high school teacher and a bachelor into his thirties, he started searching around quite seriously for Mrs. Cheap Date. Quickly tiring of spending his meager paycheck on lavish dates, he honed and polished his Cheap Date philosophy. His first dates normally consisted of a cup of coffee and conversation to see whether he was interested in trying to dazzle her with an impressive second date. These second dates were carefully orchestrated, but legendarily cheap, such as the five-cent ferry from lower Manhattan to Staten Island or an evening at night court where, as he always said, "the drama is real and the admission is free." I have seen living, happy proof that Cheap Dating is the key to finding the right person: my father eventually won the lasting love of "the most wonderful and beautiful woman to walk the earth."

Back then, he bought both cups of coffee and sprang for both ferry tokens. But that was then and this is the 90s where the term "going Dutch" is well known. The problem of finding Cheap Date spots is no longer just the concern of the male—lost hours and slimmer wallets are likewise the concern of dating women.

CHEAP DATES, though, is not just for people on the "dating scene." If you're new to the city, Boston can be a difficult and costly environment—it may intimidate you to the point of never venturing beyond your neighborhood movie theater. *CHEAP DATES* will suggest where to begin your discovery of Boston. Then again, you may have lived in the Boston area for years and never even been to the Wang Center, resigning yourself instead to renting a movie or the predictable dinner at the same old restaurant. For you, *CHEAP DATES* will reveal insider secrets, from the smart times to check out the museums to getting discount tickets for all the hottest performances.

Handy for visitors as well, *CHEAP DATES* can make tourists feel that Boston is your town too. Don't bother asking your hotel concierge for advice on where to go, unless you hope to run into every other out-of-towner in Boston.

And then there are Boston's most visible inhabitants, the one million students who flock to Beantown every year. Many come here having heard Boston is a hot city with a pulsing nightlife and culture on every street corner. But for too many students, Boston ends up as a blur of keg parties and late night binges. This kegger social scene may be every freshman's dream come true, but after two or three years it becomes every senior's monotonous nightmare. For those people who want to escape the student life for a bit, *CHEAP DATES* gives directions on how to dodge the collegiate scenes. In fact, this book is for everyone who wants to entertain, be entertained, impress and enjoy . . . and all of this while spending little money.

Many people don't realize that frugality has long been a celebrated Boston virtue—worthy of praise, not embarrassment and denial. In fact, a certain flinty thrift and parsimony is at the Yankee heart of this city. In Boston, if you've got it, you certainly don't want to flaunt it. How else can one explain the prosperity of the nation's first free libraries here in Boston, and the bargain basement trend-setting success of stores like Filene's Basement? More and more, people are taking a long hard look at the way they spend money, and when it is time to start cutting back, the entertainment budget is usually the first to feel the pinch.

As you will see, using *CHEAP DATES is very easy*. Each entry or idea includes all the necessary information to make your date virtually effortless. You'll find:

- Hours
- Phone numbers
- Directions (by public transportation and by car)
- Parking suggestions
- Prices
- The best times to go
- Helpful tips and suggestions for interesting combinations of events.

CHEAP DATES has everything needed to get you out the door, just shy of helping you put on your coat.

CHEAP DATES will take you to every corner of Boston, at every time of day. So, fall in with Boston — and fall in love.

Alexandra Ryan
Boston, Massachusetts

A NOTE ON
TRANSPORTATION

Spontaneity is a wonderful thing in dating, but when it comes to getting around, remember this maxim: Planning is everything! There is nothing worse than being picked up for a date only to have your date say, "I have a great place for us to go, but I don't know how to get there!" I cannot stress enough the importance of planning your transportation before you leave the house. If you have a car, make sure you know the directions from whence you are coming and have the correct address (in other words take this book with you!).

If you do not have a car, fear not. Boston has a very good transportation system run by the Massachusetts Bay Transit Authority (MBTA). The subway and trolley network is affectionately called the "T" by Bostonians, and is supplemented by buses, commuter trains and boats. Nearly every entry given below has suggestions for public transportation. All directions given here assume you are starting from the downtown Boston area. Read these suggestions to see if they are appropriate for you, then plan your own route. If you are stumped about how to get there without a car, let MBTA come to the rescue. Each year the MBTA puts out a fantastic reference book called *Car-Free In Boston*. It only costs about six dollars, and will be a lifesaver over and over again. If you don't have this book, the MBTA can still come to your rescue. Simply call their transportation hotline at 722-3200 or 1-800-392-6100 (24 hours a day), tell them where you are coming from and where you want to go. They will provide the route information and the average travel time. Ingenious! Remember that the T operates Monday-Saturday 5:15 a.m.-12:30 a.m. and Sundays 6:00 a.m.-12:30 a.m. Bus times vary. Be sure you know when your train or bus stops running: Cheap Date status can be ruined quickly if you have to take a $20 cab home!

Maps are another good thing to have to ensure your date goes smoothly. Boston has tons of places to get FREE maps. Most of the visitor centers provide them (the main one being on Boston Common), or try high tourist areas like South Station. If you are willing to buy a map, I've found that the best and handiest ones are *Streetwise Maps* and *Mapeasy's Guidemap to Boston*. Both are good for different reasons. Remember: it's better to look like a fool with a map in hand than to spoil a date by not knowing where you're going!

ENTERTAINING BOSTON

READER ALERT! CHEAP TICKETS!

ARTS/MAIL

I'd love to buy dinner for whoever created ARTS/BOSTON. Heck, I'd even throw in a show—I can afford it at these prices. We all know how hard it can be to get ourselves to do cultural things around Boston. It's so frustrating to know that the city is jam-packed with cool artistic offerings, yet it always seems easier to sit around your apartment and rent a movie. ARTS/BOSTON is a non-profit organization that works extremely hard to get more people to attend cultural events all over Boston. One of their most effective ventures is ARTS/MAIL. ARTS/MAIL is a simple to read (much easier than TV Guide) monthly publication that offers about 50 different activities a month for half off the regular prices.

What's the catch? Do I have to sit in a remote corner where viewing causes severe neck muscle strain? Or am I getting discount prices to all the elementary school performances in the Boston area?

The catch is that you have to order your tickets in advance, and often you must specify three dates that you can go. That's it! Not bad for what you get. I know it seems a little suspicious that they can offer half-price tickets. In fact, I had refused to purchase any myself because I was sure they would promptly hit me up for some more cash. But the truth is that ARTS/BOSTON receives large quantities of tickets at a low price and then sells them to you and me at a deep discount.

To get in on the deal, you need to call or drop a note to ARTS/BOSTON and they will send you a monthly listing of their many events. Get in on opportunities including Dance, Theater, Music, Special Events and even travel opportunities like going to New York for a Broadway performance.

ARTS/MAIL is also a great way to motivate yourself to take advantage of Boston's cultural reservoir. Each day in Boston provides a profusion of plays, dance programs and other special events—especially enjoyable at a discount price.

To receive ARTS/MAIL at your house, call or write to get put on the mailing list. *DO IT TODAY!*

ADDRESS 100 Boylston Street, Boston, MA, 02116.

PHONE 423-0372.

PRICES Half off regular prices.

BOSTIX

You like the idea of getting discount tickets, but the thought of planing ahead as far as the end of the week makes you break out in hives?

BOSTIX TO THE RESCUE!

Bostix has hundreds of same-day tickets to some of Boston's biggest productions at half off the original price.

How do I get in on this never before equaled offer?

Now Bostix has made it easier than ever with their new kiosk on Copley Square. Go to this or the other Bostix kiosk at Faneuil Hall with enough cash (or travelers checks) to purchase the tickets you want. Ask them what they have and then take your pick from a variety of shows, all half price. Be warned that they also sell full-price tickets to shows and concerts, so if your willpower is not so strong, don't go with too much cash on hand. Luckily (at least for me and my will power) Bostix doesn't accept credit cards.

No matter how hard you try, there is no one you can call at Bostix to tell you what tickets they have today. The only phone number they have will give you a recorded message of the hours and location, nothing else. Tickets can only be purchased in person if you want the half-price deal.

ADDRESS Faneuil Hall and Copley Square.

PHONE 723-5181.

HOURS Mon–Sat 10-6; Sun 11–4. *FANEUIL HALL IS CLOSED MONDAYS!*

PRICES Same-day tickets are half off the regular box office price.

DIRECTIONS The Faneuil Hall Bostix booth is easy to find, directly on the Freedom Trail and next to the original Faneuil Hall building, near Houlihan's. The Copley Square Bostix is even easier to find, on the Copley Square plaza in front of Trinity Church.
By T: (Government Center) From the Government Center stop, walk down the steps and over Congress Street to find the Bostix booth directly ahead. (Copley Square) Take Green Line to Copley. Bostix is on the corner of Boylston Street and Dartmouth Street.

THEATER

You're probably aware that Boston has a lively theater scene with several theaters and a rich variety of productions, from farce to tragedy. But did you know that many plays that later are Broadway hits have try-outs in Boston? (Many that flop on the Great White Way start out here, too.) While the theater scene is rich, so are the prices. So, to be true to form, *CHEAP DATES* has only a few recommendations. However, the local colleges and universities are a marvelous source of classical and experimental theater and the prices are much more reasonable than in the downtown theater district. (See *College Performances* section for entries.)

AMERICAN REPERTORY THEATER
Does this sound familiar?

She thinks all you want to do is sit around and watch football with a beer in hand?

He thinks your ideal man is Steven Seagal?

If so, it's time to show off your culturally sensitive side—the one that is in touch with the alternative theater of the 90s. It's time to experience the ART performances at the Loeb Drama Center in

Cambridge. ART's contemporary performances have been around for a while, but it hasn't always been quite so doable for those of us living on the cheap. Tickets usually run $18–60, and even the low-end seats are pretty great since this is a theater in the half round. There are two ways to get even cheaper tickets: one is for students only, and the other is available to everyone.

For students, ART has student rush tickets. A half hour before the curtain, all remaining tickets go on sale for $12. Only two tickets are allowed per student I.D. These tickets usually yield the less desirable seats, but if you get in line early, you can often get phenomenal seats.

Another way to get ridiculously low-priced tickets is ART's "Pay What You Can" program. Every Monday morning at 10 a.m., tickets go on sale for the Saturday matinee. Fifty tickets are put aside for whatever amount you can afford: if you're so inclined, you can buy two high-priced tickets for 5 cents. I know it sounds as if there is a catch, but there isn't. The people won't even leer at you if you go that low. "Pay What You Can" continues through the day until all 50 tickets are sold, but to be safe and get the best selection, you should get there right at 10 a.m. To find out what is showing at the Saturday matinee, simply call the box office. This is a perfect opportunity to see all the big performances for beyond cheap.

While in the neighborhood, it is imperative that you complement the date with an equally cool hangout spot such as the Nameless Coffee House, the Blacksmith House or Cafe Algiers.

ADDRESS 64 Brattle Street, Harvard Square.

PHONE Box office: 547-8300.

PRICES Regular Tickets: $18–60.
Student Rush: $12.
Most Saturday matinees are "Pay What You Can!"

DIRECTIONS ART is at the Loeb Drama Center on Brattle Street at the corner Hilliard Street From the center of Harvard Square at the Out of Town Newsstand, walk up Eliot Street and then take the first right onto Brattle Street. The Loeb Drama Center is two blocks up Brattle Street on the left side.

By T: From the Harvard Square station walk across the street to the Harvard Coop and then to the right to Church Street. Take a left on Church Street until you hit Brattle Street. Take a right onto Brattle Street and find Loeb Center on the left up few blocks.

PARKING There is parking on the street, but at performance times parking is tight. There is discount parking at University Place Parking Garage (154 Mt. Auburn Street). Make sure to take your parking ticket with you for validation at the box office.

HUNTINGTON THEATER

Owned and primarily run by Boston University (BU), the Huntington Theater is by no means a mere student theater. Everything here is purely professional. The Huntington Theater is one of the only traditional theaters in Boston that is considerate enough to dish out cheaper tickets for those of us who can't always swing the higher prices—just another example of BU's ongoing efforts to aid the cheap at heart.

Most shows at the Huntington Theater can run pretty steep (say $39 for orchestra seats on a Friday or Saturday night and $29 for everything else). But there are ways around those ugly numbers, especially if you're a student. If you are fortunate enough to be the holder of one of those costly student IDs you can get rush tickets on Tuesday, Wednesday and Thursday nights for only $12. Just show up at around 6 p.m. for the 8 p.m. performance and you can get seated in the most expensive sections for only $12. Naturally, the earlier you get there, the better seat. Make sure to bring your student ID and *CASH*. If you find yourself with tickets in hand, two hours to spare and a rumble in your stomach, you can try Ann's Restaurant down the street on the corner of Huntington and Massachusetts avenues. There you'll find extraordinarily cheap cafeteria style fare.

But say you have no student ID; you can still get cheapish tickets. The $10 tickets to Tuesday through Thursday productions are in the last row of the balcony. And trust me, I've done it. It's not that bad. Just make sure to bring extra Kleenex for those occasional nose bleeds.

If you've got a little extra time on a Wednesday afternoon, there is the 2 p.m. matinee with tickets at $18 and $30. If you're a student, you can get $5 off these prices. Not bad for a rainy day.

Although nothing quite compares to the ART's "Pay What You Can" program, I find the Huntington Theater, with its more traditional performances, more my style. In other words, when the Huntington Theater does Shakespeare, they don't do it in the nude.

ADDRESS 252 Huntington Avenue, Boston.

PHONE 266-7900.

PRICES Student Rush tickets: $12; Non-student prices: $10–50.

DIRECTIONS Located near Symphony Hall and Jordan Hall, The Huntington Theater is on Huntington Avenue between Massachusetts Avenue (Mass. Ave.) and Gainsborough Street.

By T: Take the Green Line E Train to the Symphony stop. Walk down Huntington Street and cross the street to the main entrance.

PARKING There is a convenient parking garage on Gainsborough Street at Saint Botolph Street that charges only $5 for the whole show.

NEW THEATER

A pretty impressive theater for the contemporary, low budget category, New Theater puts out about four plays a season. As the name implies, New Theater does many new scripts as well as contemporary versions of classics like Antigone. The theater is well used and conveniently located at the First and Second Church at Marlborough Street. Not too shabby for a small company. The best part about New Theater is their prices. At only $8 for students and

$10 for the rest of us, you're getting a bargain. Call them up to see what their next performances will be.

ADDRESS First and Second Church at 66 Marlborough Street, Back Bay.

PHONE 247-7388.

PRICES $10 for adults; $8 for students.

DIRECTIONS The First and Second Church is located on the beautiful and perfect-for-promenading Marlborough Street at the corner of Berkeley Street.

By T: Take the Green Line to the Arlington Street stop. Walk down Arlington Street to Marlborough Street. Take a left and walk down Marlborough Street one block to find the First and Second Church on the corner of Berkeley Street.

PARKING There is discount parking at 800 Boylston Street between Clarendon and James Streets for $5. Personally, I usually find it easier to locate meter spots on Marlborough, Berkeley or Beacon Streets if I go a little early.

MOBIUS

On the more innovative side of contemporary theater, Mobius has a long tradition of non-tradition. You can find more than theater here, with their art gallery and musical and dance performances. The theater is a funky loft space with risers for seats, and the shows are performed without a stage. (See what I mean by innovative!)

What I really admire about this stage company is that nothing is ever half-assed. They've got tons of integrity and work really hard to put on the best show they can. Most shows are Friday and Saturday nights and a Sunday matinee. Try it for a change of pace from the regular expensive theaters. Tickets are only $8 ($6 for students), so you can definitely afford to try it out.

ADDRESS 354 Congress Street, Boston.

PHONE 542-7416.

PRICES $8 for adults; $6 for students.

DIRECTIONS From Congress Street in downtown Boston, follow the street over the bridge and about three blocks past the Children's Museum on the left side.

By T: Take the Red Line to South Station then walk down Congress Street (over the bridge) for about five blocks.

PARKING There is on-street parking, but it is usually pretty sparse. You can find garage pay parking galore, but I don't suggest this. I usually take the T.

BACK ALLEY THEATER

Many different and interesting companies come to this little theater in Inman Square. Local playwrights often get to strut their stuff, while new and upcoming artists get their break. The Back Alley Theater puts on a few of their own productions each year, too. This is one of the few places in Boston where you can see a professional show for only $15 ($10 for students and seniors). Call the recording at Back Alley Theater to find out what's going on. They also have comedy at 10:30 p.m. on weekends for only $6 (see *Comedy* section for details). It's a great deal for what you get.

ADDRESS 1253 Cambridge Street, Inman Square, Cambridge.

PHONE 576-1253.

PRICES Tickets are $15; $10 for students and seniors.

DIRECTIONS The Back Alley Theater is easy to find near the corner of Cambridge and Prospect streets in the heart of Inman Square.

By T: Take the Red Line to the Central Square stop and walk up Cambridge Street to Prospect Street.

PARKING: You can almost always find parking on Cambridge Street or on surrounding streets.

BOSTON CENTER FOR THE ARTS

A chapter on theater would not be complete without a word on the Boston Center for the Arts (BCA). The BCA has three different theaters: The Black Box Stage, the BCA Theater and the Leland Theater. The BCA Theater is the largest and tends to be the site of the most traditional plays. Both the Leland and the Black Box theaters are very small and normally feature contemporary and experimental performances.

In addition to these three, there is also the Mills Gallery—one of my favorite galleries in Boston—featuring contemporary photography, sculpture, media and other art forms. Oh, I almost forgot the best part about the Mills Gallery . . . it's always *FREE*! Call ahead to be certain they are not between exhibits, and to know what to expect.

To find out what is going on at any given time, it is best to simply call the BCA's main number and ask. They will then give you the numbers of the independent companies putting on each performance. An even easier way to find out what's happening is to stop by and pick up the BCA Calendar. The Calendar covers about four months at a time so you can plan your social schedule way in advance.

ADDRESS 539 Tremont Street (at Clarendon Street) in the South End.

PHONE Main Number 426-5000.

PRICES Anywhere from *FREE* to $18.

DIRECTIONS The BCA is located at the corner of Tremont and Clarendon Streets in the heart of the South End. It is only 8 short blocks from Copley Square.

Here are a few other suggestions for cheap theater and dance tickets:

BEAU JEST MOVING THEATER at Piano Factory 791 Tremont Street, South End 437-0657.

DANCE UMBRELLA 492-7578.

NEW BROADWAY THEATER 277 Broadway, Somerville 625-1300.

NEW DANCE COMPLEX 536 Mass. Ave., Cambridge 547-9363.

NEW REPERTORY THEATER 54 Lincoln Street, Newton 332-1646.

NEW THEATER at First and Second Church, 66 Marlborough Street, Boston 247-7388.

NORA THEATRE COMPANY 12 Quincy Street, Cambridge 491-2026.

PILGRIM THEATRE 964-8918.

PUBLICK THEATRE Soldiers Field Road, Boston 720-1007 (summers only).

WHEELOCK FAMILY THEATRE 180 The Riverway, Boston 734-4760.

CLASSICAL MUSIC

It used to be that when I would imagine going to hear classical music, I would picture getting dressed up for a night out on the town with my Fairy Godmother driving the chariot, because that would be the only way I could afford the luxury of a classical concert. I have now seen the error of my ways!

ANYBODY CAN HEAR A CLASSICAL CONCERT FOR FREE OR DARN NEAR!

There may be the occasional inconvenience (like purchasing your tickets ahead of time or waiting till the last minute to get tickets), but trust me, it's worth it! If you don't yet believe me, these next entries will show you the error of *your* ways.

HANDEL & HAYDN SOCIETY

Captivatingly led by musical inspiration Christopher Hogwood, the Handel & Haydn Society (H&H) has been a leader in presenting period music as it was meant to be heard, while often adding an appropriate contemporary twist. Experiencing the H&H is like going back in time and hearing the original music with all the fervor and reverence that the original performers must have felt.

But the best part is that anyone can hear the H&H without spending too much money. It's high society without high prices. The H&H performs at three different locations: Symphony Hall, Jordan Hall and The Old South Church. At Symphony Hall the least expensive reservation ticket prices are usually $16 each, which isn't bad for what you get. But for the price of a movie and a little leg work, you can get rush tickets the day of the performance. They usually go on sale from 5 to 6 p.m. the night of the performance (1–2 p.m. for 3 p.m. performances). The catch is that only one ticket is allowed per person, so if you plan to take a date then make sure there are two of you in line to ensure you get two seats together.

The H&H usually performs at the lush Symphony Hall, but when they perform at Jordan Hall, you can get tickets an hour and a half before the show for as low as $15. If you haven't already been to Jordan Hall, then you simply must go soon! See the *College Performances* section for the New England Conservatory's frequent *FREE* concerts at Jordan Hall. Call the box office to find out when and where H&H is performing. A must-see is the H&H's performance of The Messiah during the Christmas season.

ADDRESS The H&H offices are at 300 Mass. Ave., Boston (across from Symphony Hall). Performances are at three locations:

SYMPHONY HALL: 301 Mass. Ave. (at Huntington Avenue). Symphony Hall T stop on the Green Line's E train.

JORDAN HALL: 30 Gainsborough Street (at Huntington Avenue). Located around the corner from the Symphony Hall station.

OLD SOUTH CHURCH: 645 Boylston Street (at Dartmouth Street), near the Copley T station.

PHONE H&H Box Office: 266-3605.

PRICES Ticket prices vary, but the cheapest ones are $7 for rush tickets (Symphony Hall performances only), and as low as $16 for regular performances.

BOSTON SYMPHONY ORCHESTRA

Who ever said going to hear the Boston Symphony Orchestra (BSO) was too expensive?

In 1881, Henry Lee Higginson, the founder of the BSO, made rush tickets available to anyone interested for 25 cents. God bless him. Although rush ticket prices have gone up a bit in the last hundred years, the rush ticket option still remains one of the best musical bargains in the city.

Rush tickets are a wonderful way to hear the beautiful music of the BSO led by Seiji Ozawa and numerous world-renowned guest conductors. Rush tickets are available for Tuesday, Thursday and Saturday evening performances, as well as for the Friday afternoon show. The cost is a mere $7 each and one ticket is allowed to a customer—just as with the H&H, make sure there are two of you in line to get two tickets together. Rush tickets go on sale at 9 a.m. for Friday performances and at 5 p.m. for Tuesday, Thursday and Saturday evening performances. All rush tickets are sold at the Symphony Hall West Entrance.

Another option for inexpensive tickets is the BSO Open Rehearsals. These take place on some Wednesday evenings at 7:30 ($10) and Thursday mornings at 10:30 ($9.50). If you go to an Open Rehearsal, you will be able to see a little behind-the-scenes BSO action. If you go to the morning rehearsals, there may be complimentary coffee and donuts. Not a bad way to spend a Thursday morning! These tickets are available through the ticket office Monday–Saturday, 10–6.

The third BSO bargain is "jump" seats on the second balcony. These seats are limited and have partial or obstructed views, but as long as you can hear the music who cares whether you can see all the tuba players? These tickets are also available Monday–Saturday, 10–6 at Symphony Hall.

So that's it! How much more convincing do you need? The BSO is accessible to everybody. These three options should give you more than enough opportunities to attend the symphony. And just because Seiji wears a tuxedo to each performance does not mean that you have to. But keep in mind that people do tend to "dress" for this event. You and your date may really enjoy having a spiffy night out in high society Boston.

ADDRESS 301 Mass. Ave., Boston.

PHONE 266-1492 for information; 266-1200 for tickets.

PRICES The BSO's cheapest tickets are $7–10 (some suckers pay as much as $67!).

DIRECTIONS Symphony Hall is located on Mass. Ave. at Huntington Avenue near the Christian Science Mother Church.

By T: The T is the best idea since the Symphony stop is directly below Symphony Hall and parking is very difficult on performance nights.

PARKING If you do decide to drive, parking can be tricky. But with all of the meter spots on the side streets, a little patience, and maybe a bit of walking, you should find parking. *GO EARLY!*

THE GARDNER MUSEUM CONCERTS

If you haven't yet gone to one of the Gardner Museum's fabulous concerts, it should be your next weekend activity. The Gardner Museum, renowned for the incredible private collection of Isabella

Stewart Gardner's art, also has some of Boston's best bargain music. The concerts are every Saturday and Sunday featuring mostly classical music, but often a contemporary piece, too.

Ticket prices are $15 for adults, $9 for students and seniors and only $4 for members. Concert tickets include the price of admission to the museum, and are a real bargain as long as you plan enough time on your date to visit the whole museum. If you think about it this way, concert tickets are really only $8 if you take out the $7 admission fee. All in all, not a bad price for two hours of heavenly music in a beautiful concert hall and then hours of pleasure in the rest of the museum. The concerts are held in the Tapestry Room with its ancient tile floors and fine old paneling—not to mention a whole lot of gorgeous tapestries.

My advice would be to get to the Gardner Museum early for two reasons. One, so that you can get tickets; non-members can't reserve tickets and they go pretty quickly. Two, to get the good seats up front where you can see and hear much better. Concerts start at 1:30 p.m., so you should get there at 1:00, get tickets, save seats with coats, then take a stroll around the second floor. Make sure to save a couple of rooms of the museum for after the concert. Since you're paying for museum admission price with the ticket, you may as well get your money's worth!

Falling in love with the performances at the Gardner Museum is all the more reason to become a member. Admission to concerts is $4 for members and museum admission is *FREE*—not a bad deal. The Gardner Museum also has performances at other times; you can find out about them by calling their concert line. If you're a member, you naturally get many special privileges including the $4 concerts, ability to make reservations at performances and at the scrumptious Gardner Cafe, and the monthly Gardner Calendar filled with receptions, concerts and special exhibits. A single membership is only $40 a year and $60 a year for two or a family. It's really a bargain if you love the Gardner Museum and want to take advantage of all their great offerings.

ADDRESS 280 The Fenway, Boston.

PHONE Concert line is 734-1359.

HOURS Concerts are Saturday and Sunday at 1:30.

PRICES Concerts are $15 (includes admission to museum); $9 for college students and seniors; $7 for youths 12-17; $4 for members.

DIRECTIONS Located on the curvy Fenway Street that follows the Charles River, the Gardner Museum is between Simmons College and he Museum of Fine Arts (MFA), with a grassy park adjacent.

By T: Take the Green Line E to the Ruggles/Museum stop. Walk down Museum Road past the MFA toward the green of the Fens. Bear left and it's on the corner of Fenway Street and Evans Way Street.

PARKING Meter parking normally isn't too difficult on the side streets surrounding the Gardner Museum. But if you are patient, you may even find an unmetered spot on curbs surrounding the grassy park next door. Otherwise, there is pay parking close by at the MFA.

FRENCH LIBRARY

In its ongoing effort to better educate Bostonians to the civility of the French, the beautiful and newly restored French Library provides a few classical concerts each week. Weeknight concerts usually begin at 6:15 and a reception often follows. The cost for these concerts is about $8. If you want to enjoy *un concert français*, but don't want to dish out the 8 bucks, then try their *Musique à Midi* on Wednesdays. These concerts start at noon and are *FREE*. The easiest way to find out about all of the library's programs is to become a member and receive a monthly listing of their activities. Membership for one year is $40. If French isn't your forte and membership is not in your future, then call them at 266-4351 or drop by to pick up a schedule of events. Don't worry, they will answer all your questions in English, but with a heavy French accent.

ADDRESS 53 Marlborough Street, Back Bay.

PHONE 266-4351.

HOURS Weeknight concerts times vary, but usually are at about 6:15 p.m. *Musique à Midi* begins at . . . noon.

PRICES   Evening concerts: $8 (reception included).
        Noon concerts: *FREE*.

DIRECTIONS The French Library is on the corner of Berkeley and Marlborough streets a block away from the Public Garden.

By T: The closest T station is Arlington. From the exit walk down Arlington Street towards the Public Garden and take a left onto Marlborough Street. The library is one block down on the right.

PARKING Meter parking is available out front. Members receive parking benefits at 500 Boylston Street.

TRINITY CHURCH

What better place to hear the notes inspired by God than at this beautiful church built over 120 years ago. Somehow when you hear classical music performed at Trinity Church, it seems silly to listen to classical music in any other forum. The building is fine for acoustics, but the real treat is the beauty of the surroundings. It feels as if you're in heaven listening to God's angels. An afternoon at Trinity Church could make a convert of just about anyone.

Each Friday afternoon brings the well-known half-hour *FREE* organ concert at the Trinity. A half-hour organ concert is a great way to begin the weekend.

If you want to hear their beautiful choral music, you can attend a special Sunday morning Music Worship Service. The music begins at 10:45 and then continues throughout the service. These special services only happen twice a month, so make sure to call first or get a schedule.

Trinity Church also has a host of other heart-tingling concerts that should become a regular part of your entertainment. Call to be put on their mailing list.

ADDRESS Copley Square.

PHONE 536-0944 or 326-1520.

HOURS Friday concerts at 12:15. Sunday services with music is at 11:00 (music begins at 10:45). Call to find out which Sundays have this special service.

PRICES Friday and Sunday performances are *FREE*. Some evenings Trinity Church performances charge admission of about $10.

DIRECTIONS Trinity is the larger church in the heart of Copley Square on Boylston and Dartmouth streets.

By T: Take the Green Line to Copley Square and you're there!

PARKING Parking is extremely difficult in Copley Square. Try some of the side streets and be alert for people leaving spots. Parking on Sunday mornings between 10:30 and 11 is usually a bit easier.

Here are a few other sources for cheap classical music:

> **BOSTON CHAMBER MUSIC SOCIETY** at Sanders Theater and Jordan Hall 422-0086.
> **FEDERAL RESERVE BANK OF BOSTON CONCERT SERIES** (lunchtime concerts) 600 Atlantic Avenue, Boston 973-3453.
> **KING'S CHAPEL** (lunchtime concerts and more) 58 Tremont Street, Boston 227-2155.
> **OLD WEST ORGAN SOCIETY** at Old West Church, 131 Cambridge Street, Beacon Hill 739-1340 & 508-744-0245.
> **ST. PAUL'S CATHEDRAL** (lunchtime concerts) 138 Tremont Street, Boston 482-5800.

LIVE JAZZ TONIGHT

LENNIE'S

NO COVER • DANCING ALLOWED

LIVE MUSIC

Boston has long been at the forefront of the contemporary music scene. The Hub's got music to suit everyone's taste. We've got jazz, rock, blues, heavy metal, country and even karaoke. You can listen, dance, clap, sing along and even sing it all by yourself. If you think Boston is only good for the classical stuff and you've got to go to New York City for hipper tunes, you're mistaken.

WALLY'S CAFE

When it comes to hearing blues and jazz in the setting it's supposed to be heard, Wally's in the South End is it. First of all, there's no cover—ever. If you're a true Cheap Dater you need not read further. But it seems worth mentioning that the music is fantastic with sets that will leave you deaf and craving more. It is somewhat addicting, but if you're going to take up a habit, this is a good one.

Most evenings the place gets so wild that you can feel the foundation shake as performers and listeners alike get down and dirty. When you hear the incredible music that explodes from this veritable hole in the wall, then you'll realize you've found yourself a golden egg. Wally's is great for blues, but is also known for jazz, funk rock, soul and much more. Each night of the week offers a different taste, and each set presents a variety of styles. Wally's should be the first place you go to find excellent authentic blues and jazz in this fair and far too yuppiefied city of ours. It's not fancy, it's not overpriced and it's not even clean . . . but blues ain't supposed to be. Wally's has got more packed into their joint than most of the rest of the city. Tables are often hard to come by, but stake one out and then stay the evening, paying only for the reasonably priced beer. Since Wally's is small, people tend to share tables. Don't be shy; it's a great way to meet people.

ADDRESS 427 Mass. Ave., South End.

PHONE 424-1408.

PRICES Cover is always *FREE*. Beers and drinks are very reasonable. If you occupy a table, make sure to order often enough to keep the waitresses happy.

DIRECTIONS: Although Wally's is located right on Mass. Avenue, it is easy to miss. Near Columbus Avenue across from the Mass. Ave. station, a small Budweiser sign modestly reveals Wally's. Don't be daunted, just walk right in.

By T: The Orange Line's Mass. Ave. station is across the street. If the Green Line is your preference, you can take it to either the Hynes Convention Center or Symphony Hall and take an inexpensive taxi or even walk with a few companions.

PARKING: Street parking is your best (and only) bet. Make sure to lock up in this neighborhood.

THE MIDDLE EAST

Besides being a tasty and cheap restaurant (see page 92 for more details) the Middle East is very popular with those up on the local music scene in Boston. Every night there is live music and very often it is free or darn near. The restaurant has two sections (separated by an Indian restaurant in the middle) and then there is a basement where there are bigger shows (and bigger prices). The bakery usually has live music for free or close to it, while there is normally a cover charge of $5–12 to get downstairs or to the other side. From time to time a cover charge to the downstairs will also get you into TT the Bears next door. Call their hotline to see who's on and how much it'll cost you. In general drinks are pretty reasonable. Beers run $2.50–3 and you can get pitchers of beer for about $10. The Middle East makes for a great combo dinner and live music date any night of the week.

ADDRESS 472 and 480 Mass. Ave., Central Square, Cambridge.

PHONE 492-9181. For music info: 492-5162 (then press 1 about a hundred times).

HOURS Open every night till 2 a.m. Shows start at all different times.

PRICES Prices vary from **FREE** to about $12.

DIRECTIONS From Boston take Mass. Ave. over the Mass. Ave. Bridge for about a mile to find the Middle East on the left side of the street.

By T: Take Red Line to Central Square station. Walk south on Mass. Ave. for about two blocks to find the Middle East on the right side of the street.

PARKING There is usually some street parking available. Try the side streets.

PASSIM

Passim is very well-known to those who love folk music. It's cheap and fun, and another bonus is that it's smoke and alcohol free. Ain't that refreshing? Many famous people have started out at Passim—have you heard of Tom Rush and Suzanne Vega? Nowadays you can hear lots of up-and-coming groups, like Chris Trapper and the Pushstars, who won't be playing for this cheap much longer. The cover charge varies, but usually hovers around the $8 mark. Some nights are "in the round" where a few musicians and poets take turns performing. Tuesday nights are usually open mike-nights for $3; and thanks to the lack of alcohol served on the premises, they tend to be a little better than open-mike nights at other places. You can get a dessert or a cup of tea or coffee at Passim, and reservations are accepted. If there is a show you wanted to see here, but you couldn't make it, tune into WERS (Emerson College's radio station), where they often broadcast live sets from Passim.

ADDRESS 47 Palmer Street, Harvard Square.

PHONE 492-7679.

HOURS Shows start at various times and the club stays open till about 3 a.m.

PRICES Tickets range from $3–12.

DIRECTIONS From Memorial Drive, take JFK Boulevard into the Square, then a left onto Eliot Street at the Harvard Coop. Palmer Street is the first right. Passim is below the Globe Corner Bookstore on the corner of Church Street.

THE TAM O' SHANTER

The Tam has one of the widest varieties of musical genres in Boston. They feature every kind of music imaginable and they often add a twist: folk, alternative rock, country rock, jazz ensembles, hearty blues, and open Jazz and Blues nights where you too could have your stage debut. The cover charge is between $3 and $6, and almost always guarantees a good show. Some nights you can visit the Tam and come out with pounding eardrums, and on others it can be very mellow with more opportunity to chat with your date. Thursday, Friday and Saturday nights are much rowdier than the rest of the week. Sunday and Monday nights are particularly pleasant if some jazz, blues and conversation are what you're in the mood for. It's a nice way to start the week.

Shows usually begin at 10:15, after dinner service is over. A pleasurable and relatively Cheap Date can be a savory dinner at the restaurant and then some lively music. You don't even have to find new seats. Call to find out what music is on tap.

ADDRESS 1648 Beacon Street, Brookline.

PHONE 277-0982.

HOURS Dinner is served 5–1:30. Music starts at 10:15–10:30 and goes until about 1:30.

PRICES Cover charge is $5–6, depending on the band.

DIRECTIONS Located right on Beacon Street near the intersection with Washington Street, the Tam is about half a mile between Coolidge Corner and Cleveland Circle.

By T: The Green Line's C train stops in front of the Tam.

PARKING On a weekend you are running the risk of having to walk a few blocks, but otherwise you can usually park right out in front of the Tam.

THE WONDER BAR

Although I was really sad to see Local 186 (formally Bunratty's) leave our midst, I have to say The Wonder Bar is about the best thing that's ever happened to the Allston/Brighton area. If you've gone by it, you can attest to the success The Wonder Bar has experienced. Besides having a total face lift putting The Wonder Bar on par with Sonsie and Cafe MoJo, The Wonder Bar has got something that the rest don't: live jazz seven nights a week. And I mean good jazz. Every night you can mellow out to great music and fine food in this glamorous dark wood and gilded ceiling setting. What's even better than great jazz in a beautiful setting, is great jazz in a beautiful setting that's always *FREE*! It almost seems too good to last.

A line starts to form outside The Wonder Bar at around 10 on Fridays and Saturdays, so you may want to go early and get a good seat. The Wonder Bar also has a fabulous Jazz Brunch daily that is simply unmatched. Another bonus of The Wonder Bar is the food. The menu, designed by chef extraodinaire Kate Painter, is a wonderful mix of classical and haute cuisine with salads, soups, entrées, peanut butter and jelly sandwiches, et al at very modest prices. Beers and drinks are about as reasonable as the food.

If you haven't yet been to The Wonder Bar, it's time. Keep in mind that there is a dress code: no baseball hats or torn clothing are allowed. In general, people tend to dress a little nicer here than at some of the neighborhood's other establishments.

ADDRESS 186 Harvard Avenue, Brighton.

PHONE 351-2665.

HOURS 5 p.m.–2 a.m. Hours change frequently, so call ahead for brunch hours.

PRICES *NO COVER CHARGE* Drinks: $3–4.

DIRECTIONS The Wonder Bar's beautiful facade is located on Harvard Avenue near the intersection of Commonwealth Avenue across from Marty's Liquors.

By T: Take the Green Line B train to Harvard Avenue and turn right. The Wonder Bar will be a few doors down Harvard Avenue on your right side.

PARKING Parking in Allston is no picnic. If you plan to drive, go early and find spots on surrounding streets.

HARPER'S FERRY

Although it isn't always cheap, Harper's Ferry is a sure bet for some rollicking R&B. Once you enter the door into this gigantic barn-like establishment, it's easy to forget you are in Allston. The crowd seems a little out of place in this neighborhood so often overrun by students. In fact, you might expect to see John Travolta and Debra Winger cavort on Harper's dance floor; it's too bad they don't have an electric bull.

Not only is Harper's Ferry reliable for a raucous time, but its is well known for stocking some major performers.

For the bigger shows, tickets run up to $10 ahead of time and $12 at the door. Sunday through Wednesday, when you can expect anything from open mike to smaller bands, cover charge is only $2. The other nights, that always pack a great show, cover is $6. Bands go on at about 9:30, usually performing till about 2 a.m. If you just want to stop in some time without paying a fee, you can get in after about 12:30 a.m. without paying a cover. Last call is usually at 1:50. Harper's Ferry also has a lot of pool tables and dart boards if the music isn't sending you. Call to see who's on, or you can drive by and check out their marquee. Then *GO*! You'll be back for sure.

ADDRESS 158 Brighton Avenue, Allston.

PHONE 254-9743.

HOURS Open noon–2 a.m. Music starts around 9:30–10.

PRICES Mon–Wed $2; Thur–Sat $6. Big shows are $10–12.

DIRECTIONS Easy to find, Harper's Ferry's big blue facade and marquee are on Brighton Avenue near the intersection with Harvard Avenue. It is a few doors down from Blanchard's Liquors and across the street from The Kels.

By T: There are a variety of trains and buses (Buses 58 and 66) that stop around Harper's Ferry. The most common way is by taking the Green Line B train to the Harvard Avenue stop. Walk one block down Harvard Avenue to Brighton Avenue and take a left onto Brighton Avenue. Harper's Ferry will be a couple of doors down on your left.

PARKING Be very careful parking anywhere around here. It seems that most Allstonians make their living off of car towing. Harvard and Brighton avenues are the best for street parking, or try farther up Brighton Avenue toward Union Square.

BLACK ROSE

The Black Rose, with locations in Faneuil Hall and Harvard Square, is a step above other joints. Although things can occasionally get just as rowdy here as elsewhere, the Black Rose manages to provide good live music in a more serene atmosphere. It is clean, less smoky and has a generally agreeable clientele. You can expect music of all kinds, but especially Irish. Anything from traditional folk to covers of U2 can be expected. Beers are reasonably priced (shots are outrageously expensive), and you can get cheap Irish food (is there any other?). At the Faneuil Hall location, the Black Rose has a versatility that most other clubs lack. It's always fun at night, but if you stop by after work or while shopping in the area, it can be an equally entertaining, mellow spot. Not only is the Black Rose a good late evening place, but it also serves as a soothing after work (or play) spot, too.

Private parties at the Faneuil Hall location are a great way to get all your friends together without paying too much or trashing your own place. You can rent the upstairs, and guests can purchase drinks at the large bar on that floor. It is also a nice way of raising money for a charity by charging a modest admission at the door.

ADDRESS   160 State Street, Faneuil Hall.
                        50 Church Street, Harvard Square.
PHONE Faneuil Hall: 742-2286. Harvard Square: 492-8630.

HOURS The Black Rose is open 365 days a year, 11 a.m.–2 a.m. Last call is usually 1:45.

PRICES The standard cover charge is $5. Beers are a reasonable $3-4.

DIRECTIONS Faneuil Hall: On State Street near the Custom House Tower, the Black Rose is in the heart of Faneuil Hall.

Harvard Square: Church Street is perpendicular to Mass. Ave. and runs through to Brattle Street. The Black Rose is halfway down on the left side.

By T: Faneuil Hall: From the Government Center station, walk down the giant steps to Faneuil Hall and follow above directions.

Harvard Square: From the Mass. Ave. exit at Harvard Square on the Red Line, Church Street will be in front of you near The Body Shop. Walk down 1-1/2 blocks to find the Black Rose on your left.

PARKING Please don't drive to either location. If you do, I take no responsibility for the money spent on garage parking!

THE HOUSE OF BLUES

Although The House of Blues can be rather expensive, it too can become a Cheap Date with a little caution. First of all, The House of Blues is certain to impress with its chic Harvard Square location and its excellent shows. But the key to an enjoyable Cheap Date is to go on weeknights. The cover is low, usually around $5, and the crowd is thinned out (as is the haze of smoke). The House of Blues diligently packs each night with an impressive lineup of local and national performers. As with most blues joints, there is a genuine sense of pride in one's art form that permeates each performer, guest and employee. Even the art work that covers the walls of the House of Blues is wildly impressive.

Because of The House of Blues' reputation and famous co-owner Dan Aykroyd, it is able to consistently book big names.

Whereas at some smaller, less popular joints a weeknight may feature the headwaiter and cook playing spoons, The House of Blues manages a dazzling show every night of the week. Call ahead to see who's on and what ticket prices are. If you're in the neighborhood, pick up their six-week schedule of shows.

If you are opposed to waiting in line before the show starts, have dinner at their downstairs restaurant. The cuisine is classic southern foods. But don't be frightened; it's quite tasty. If you go to The House of Blues on a weeknight, might I suggest Grendel's Bar Appetizer Specials for $1.50? Also 5–7 and 9–11, Monday–Thursday (only 5–7 on Fridays), you can get any one of their many appetizers for only $1.50 if you're ordering alcohol drinks. It's a bargain you don't want to miss. Also, considering the drinks at Grendel's cost half those at The House of Blues, I would suggest you get your fill while at Grendel's Bar.

If you find yourself getting into southern cuisine, I think you should seek counseling . . . no, just kidding. What I was going to say is that you should try their Sunday Gospel Brunch. It is unmatched. Fried okra, grits and catfish, anyone?

ADDRESS 96 Winthrop Street, Harvard Square.

PHONE 491-2583. Call for schedule of shows.

HOURS Open every day at 11:30, closes at 1 a.m. on weekdays and 2 a.m. on weekends and Thursdays.

PRICES Weekend prices can run from $10 to $28, but the weekday shows are much cheaper at $6–$7. The drink prices are not outrageous, but on the other hand not cheap, with beers running $2.75–4.

DIRECTIONS It's usually hard to miss the lines and commotion outside of The House of Blues (not to mention the blue neon signs). But Winthrop Street is slightly tucked back as it runs between JFK Boulevard to Eliot Street. The House of Blues is across Winthrop Street from the entrance to Grendel's Den.

By T: Harvard Square and the T are always a great combination. From the Harvard Square station take a left onto JFK Boulevard and follow it straight across Mt. Auburn Street to Winthrop Street. Take a right onto Winthrop Street and The House of Blues will soon be on your left.

PARKING The typical Harvard Square nightmare parking situation is inevitable. Weeknights are easier to park on the street. Go early and be patient. Try some of the side streets farther out of the Square near Mt. Auburn Cemetery.

RATHSKELLER

I almost can't believe that I'm adding the Rathskeller (the Rat) to a book with my name on it. As an undergraduate at BU and living in Kenmore Square, I always thought of the Rat as a sinister joint where people went in and never came out—I used to get a little nervous just walking by it in broad daylight. But now that I'm a big girl (sort of) I've learned that the Rat is actually a place of grand repute (sort of). Here are the facts: many great bands played at the Rat in their early days including The Cars and Aerosmith; and it's cheap! Local lore even says that the Rat was the first place The Police ever played in America.

The Rat is pretty hard core and I've learned to love it. It's got two levels. The upper level is always *FREE* and local bands play upstairs for exposure. Downstairs is where the concerts are—as is the cover charge—but it's only $4–9. Some pretty great bands play down there.

The Rat has extremely cheap beers; we're talking Black Label for a buck. It's also the kind of place that takes away beer bottles at a certain point to deter belligerent patrons. But don't let me frighten you, it's a really hip place. Get decked out! Drag out those leather pants! Don those chains! Have fun! You may be able to say years down the road, "I saw the Flying Squirrels at the Rat before they were big!"

ADDRESS 528 Commonwealth Avenue, Kenmore Square.

PHONE 536-2750.

HOURS Open till 2 a.m.

PRICES Upstairs is *FREE*. Shows are $3–9.

DIRECTIONS On the non-river side of Kenmore Square, the Rat is nestled in between India Quality Restaurant (good food and cheap if you're in the mood) and Strawberries.

By T: The Rat is located directly above the Kenmore T stop on the Green Line.

PARKING You can always find a parking spot somewhere; it's just a matter of how far you'll have to walk afterward. Try Bay State Road.

> *Here are a few other spots that have great live music at low prices:*
>
> **11TH CHAPTER SALOON** 366A Somerville 628-4300.
>
> **BAY TOWER ROOM** 60 State Street, Boston 723-1666 (dress nicely).
>
> **BURKE'S** 808 Huntington Avenue, Boston 232-2191.
>
> **THE MIDWAY CAFE** 3496 Washington Avenue, Jamaica Plain 524-9038.
>
> **THE NAMELESS COFFEEHOUSE** 3 Church Street, Harvard Square 864-1630.
>
> **PARADISE** 969 Commonwealth Avenue, Brighton 562-8800.
>
> **PLOUGH AND STARS** 912 Mass. Ave., Cambridge 492-9653.
>
> **TOAD** 1920 Mass. Ave., Porter Square 497-4950.

COMEDY

Boston usually has a wealth of comedy clubs. The problem is that they tend to open and close with the frequency of cheap restaurants. Also, it's a crap shoot; some nights you can go there and laugh until your diaphragm has had it, other nights you can walk out with nothing gained except smoke-filled clothes. Although there is very little way to cut down the risk of a bad show, you can at least cut the price a little by going during the week. On weeknights, most comedy clubs have a number of performers who only stand up for 5–10 minutes each. This way you're pretty much guaranteed to see someone you think is hysterical, and those you can't stand are not around long. Besides, even bad comedy makes for good conversation after the show. The following comedy clubs are ones that seem most solid and promising.

Note: Keep in mind that a comedy club isn't exactly a Disney movie; much of the language and content can be rather raunchy. Try to forecast whether you and your date are going to be comfortable in this kind of atmosphere.

NICK'S COMEDY STOP

Nick's Comedy Stop is one of Boston's hippest comedy clubs. You won't find any of the snug qualities of other smaller clubs, but you will get bright lights, lots of people and more than just comedy. Nick's has two levels, one for comedy and the other for dancing. This rules out any risk of wasting your money on bad comedians, because you can always hit the dance floor if the show isn't working for you. Both levels have an excess of bars that are fully stocked and ready to serve.

The weekends pack an hour and a half with some of the country's better known comics. The weekdays have smaller names, but usually the laughs are just as big. For your first time, try a lower-priced weeknight show and then see if you want to move up to the big-time weekends. **Warning:** As far as risqué material goes, Nick's has yielded some of the raciest I've heard.

ADDRESS 100 Warrenton Street, Theater District.

PHONE 482-0930 Box Office: 1-800-441-JOKE.

HOURS On weekdays shows start at 8:30 and last two hours. Weekend shows begin at 8:30 and 10; these shows are 1-1/2 hours.

PRICES Mon–Wed $6; Thur and Sun $8; Fri–Sat $12.

DIRECTIONS Located on Warrenton Street, Nick's has a giant sign reading "Comedy Club," making it difficult to miss. From Boylston Street next to the Common take a right onto Tremont Street, then your first right onto Eliot Street and then your first left onto Warrenton Street.

By T: Taking the T is always the smartest when venturing into the Theater District. Take the Green Line to the Boylston Street stop. You will be on the corner of Tremont and Boylston streets; from there follow above directions.

PARKING If you are really patient and get there early enough to look hard, you can find street parking. Otherwise, there is pay parking everywhere. However, parking in a lot is a sin against all that is considered holy by Cheap Daters.

COMEDY CONNECTION

The Comedy Connection, now located in Faneuil Hall, books some of Boston's biggest comedy acts. Prices tend to get a little high on weekends depending on the comedian, but it's still possible to get in for cheap. Sunday through Wednesday nights usually have general admission for just $8. Another way to get in on the big shows for less is to look for coupons: magazines, newspapers, coupon books and those annoying people who hand out stuff on the streets often have great coupons for Comedy Connection.

One of the more interesting nights at Comedy Connection is when they have a hypnotist. This is really weird and authentic humor. Don't be shy—volunteer to go on stage to prove to yourself that it's not a hoax.

Because the Comedy Connection has such a great parking deal, it's worth it to go early and have dinner. Try Artu in the North End for, you guessed it, Italian food!

ADDRESS 245 Quincy Market, Faneuil Hall.

PHONE 248-9700.

HOURS Weeknights there is one show at 8. On Friday and Saturday nights there are usually two shows at 8 and 10.

ADMISSION General admission on weeknights is about $8. On Friday and Saturday admission is $10–30.

DIRECTIONS On the upper level of Quincy Marketplace by Faneuil Hall. Go to the rotunda in the middle of the main building and up the stairs to find the line for Comedy Connection.

PARKING The Comedy Connection has whopper of a deal on parking at the corner of State and Broad Streets. If you park after 4 p.m. on weekdays, and all day on weekends, it's only $4 (that's $4 for the whole night—not an hour!)

IMPROVBOSTON AT BACK ALLEY THEATER

The Back Alley Theater is well known for its offbeat theater productions, but now they have the IMPROVBOSTON troupe to tout about. Friday and Saturday nights are the best shows, but there is usually a wacky standup show on Wednesdays for a mere $5. The theater is charming; in the heart of Inman Square, and the price is right. The variety and schedule changes often, so call their recorded message for details. You will also get to hear what productions are going on at this unique little theater.

ADDRESS 1253 Cambridge Street, Inman Square, Cambridge.

PHONE 576-1253.

HOURS Times vary, so call for details.

PRICES Sunday–Thursday $8; Friday and Saturday tickets go up to $12. There are also special weekend rates ($10) for students and seniors.

DIRECTIONS The Back Alley Theater is in the heart of Inman Square on Cambridge Street near Prospect Street.

By T: Take the Red Line to Central Square and walk up Prospect Street for about ten minutes to Cambridge Street.

PARKING You can almost always find parking on Cambridge Street or surrounding streets.

Also try:

AKU AKU COMEDY CAMPUS 109 Brookline Avenue, Boston 267-6626.

DICK DOHERTY'S COMEDY VAULT 124 Boylston Street, Boston 267-6626.

LYRICAL STAGE 140 Clarendon Street, Boston 437-7172.

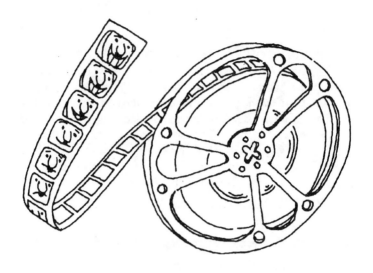

FILMS

Dinner and a movie is probably the most common date in the book (not this book, of course). It used to be a safe, convenient and cheap alternative to those other costly dates. Now, dinner and a movie *is* the costly date. Not only is it expensive, but you often find yourself in an embarrassing situation watching an uncomfortable sex scene with a crowd of unsavory youths cheering it on.

Luckily, there is an alternative. The next few entries will convince you that there is hope for the classic movie date. There are still nice theaters out there that don't cater to the giant cineplex mentality of packing in patrons like so many cattle. You'll see.

But before you read on, there is one more important point to make. Did you know that it is a Cheap Date sin to buy refreshments at those overpriced cinema counters? It's almost considered blasphemy to even mention them. The solution is simple; called:

BYOG

That is, **Bring Your Own Goodies**. All you need do is swing by a local convenience store on your way to the theater—it doesn't even have to be a particularly cheap store. While at the convenience store, you stock up on as many goodies as you'd like—don't forget the drink. *THEN* you may proceed to the theater. Now wasn't that painless.

BELMONT CINEMA

If you're familiar with the Fresh Pond Theater, you'll find the quaint and wonderfully cheap Belmont Cinema close by. A sixth sense tells me that little has changed here in the past forty years, including both the ticket prices and the woman who sells them. Also, the movies they show are always relatively current and they're good films unlikely to offend anyone. And the movie changes each week: I find myself there just about every week with my $4 in hand and a big smile one my face knowing that I could be spending double that just down the street. (They also have a refreshments counter that almost passes the BYOG rule. You are allowed to purchase something here and still call yourself a Cheap Dater—but I think you're better off importing your goodies.)

The Belmont Cinema lists its movies in the newspaper; but they usually have 7 and 9 showings every night. Call to be certain.

ADDRESS 376 Trapelo Road, Belmont.

PHONE 484-1706.

PRICES General admission is $4.

DIRECTIONS From Boston, take Route 2 toward Belmont to Belmont Street. Follow Belmont Street to Trapelo Road. Follow Trapelo Road for about two miles and find the Belmont Cinema on the left side.

PARKING Parking is available on the street and is usually ample. Don't you love these suburbs!

CAPITOL THEATER

I adore this theater. It's what a big movie house should be. There are huge screens, plenty of seats, reasonably priced refreshments (plus tables like a little cafe) and *SIX* cinemas. Just as the Belmont Theater provides good films for adults and kids, the Capitol Theater shows many children's films during the day and then puts on more adult films at night.

Admittedly my favorite part is the $4 price, but the decor is pretty cool too. An authentic old movie house, this theater has retained its 1920s feel while providing comfortable chairs and all the conveniences too! A godsend.

If you know a child you'd like to take to the movies, this is the place to go because before 6 p.m. children get in for $2.50. If you do the math you'll see that the two of you can go to the movies for $6.50. That's less than one person at a regular theater. *YIPPEE!* You can also buy a book of five tickets for $18. At a regular theater that would be about $38—a $20 savings. (I swear I didn't even have to use a calculator for any of these calculations.) Arlington Center is also great place to cruise around before or after the show. A good place for a little ice cream.

ADDRESS 204 Mass. Ave., Arlington.

PHONE 648-4340.

PRICES $4 for adults; $2.50 for children and all shows before 6 p.m.; $3 for seniors. A book of five tickets is $18.

DIRECTIONS It's so easy. Get on Mass. Ave. toward Cambridge and follow it to Arlington Center. The Capitol Theater is on the left. For other directions, give them a call at the theater.

PARKING Parking is available on the surrounding streets.

SOMERVILLE THEATER

When this old stage theater in Davis Square isn't hosting a live concert, they show second-run movies. The films are usually really fantastic, the prices very low, and the neighborhood is always fun. Movies are normally shown at 7 and 9 (call to be certain) and are always $2.50. It's a waste to go to this neighborhood and just take in a movie when there are so may other great things to do here. Complement the movie with a meal at one of the many great restaurants like The Rosebud Cafe, Redbones or Mikes Restaurant (see *Eating Out* section for details). There is also a great coffee house next door to the theater called Someday Cafe; the perfect place for a cup of java and conversation.

ADDRESS 55 Davis Square, Somerville.

PHONE 625-5700.

HOURS Usually 7 and 9 p.m. showings, but call ahead.

ADMISSION Movies are only $2.50!

DIRECTIONS From Mass. Ave. after Porter Square take a right onto Day Street and then a left onto Elm Street at Davis Square.

PARKING Parking is pretty easy in this neighborhood with street parking and municipal lots all around.

QUESTION: Do you know any place you can go to the movies for $2?

ANSWER: DEDHAM COMMUNITY CINEMA

Located in lovely Dedham Center, this little theater has much to boast about: with just two cinemas, they manage to show about six different movies every day. The films are a mix of children's (shown during the day), and big-hit films usually a week or two after they've been in the major theaters. So wait, read the reviews, then visit the Dedham Community Theater with the satisfaction of knowing you are seeing a great movie for only $5!

What could be better, you ask?

Well, if you go to the first showing of the day, you can get in for only $2. *TWO DOLLARS!* That's just silly cheap.

ADDRESS 578 High Street, Dedham.

PHONE 326-1463.

PRICES $5 for adults; kids and seniors $3; $2 for anyone going to the first show of the day.

DIRECTIONS From Boston take the VFW Parkway to Route 1 towards Westwood. At the Mattress Discounters in Dedham, take a right. At the first set of lights, High Street, take a left and the theater will be on your right.

PARKING There is plenty of on-site parking at Dedham Community Theater.

THE LEXINGTON FLICK

Located in one of the quaintest neighborhoods in the Boston area, the Lexington Flick is the perfect excuse to get yourself out of the city. You can have a nice dinner at one of the many local restaurants (I'm partial to Bel Canto across the street), enjoy a cup of coffee at Coffee Connection, then stop in to CVS to stock up on your movie-time goodies. Or if you're not as hungry as I usually am, just do one of these things.

The Flick is a smallish theater that runs about seven films every day, including first-run films, children's movies and sleeper hits. They choose carefully to provide only the most acclaimed and entertaining films. This theater has a wonderful homey feeling that is perfect for the rainy day movie excursion. And if that won't get you out to Lexington, this might: all shows before 6 and *ALL* shows on Wednesdays are only $3. And if you can't make it to one of those, the highest priced shows are only $5. Can't beat that.

ADDRESS 1794 Mass. Ave., Lexington.

PHONE 861-6161.

PRICES Adults $5; children and seniors $3.50.

DIRECTIONS From Boston you can always take Mass. Ave. all the way out there if you've got time to kill. But if you want to get there efficiently, take Route 2 to Lexington/Mass. Ave. Continue on Mass. Ave. to Lexington Center and find the theater on your left.

PARKING Parking is available all around.

MUSEUM OF FINE ARTS

The Museum of Fine Arts (MFA) consistently provides quality films for members, non-members, art lovers and artephobics (if I may make the word up). Not only does the MFA have fascinating and diverse movies, but it has the best theater in Boston. You won't find brats yelling out lewd things or people throwing popcorn here. But if you're thinking it's a bunch of stuffy old museum types with pipes and brooches, you're wrong! This happens to be one of the most popular theaters for people of all types. The seats are amazingly comfortable and perfect for snuggling up to your companion—just try not to fall asleep.

The film selection varies from sensual films of love in modern times, to ethnic films from around the world, to docudramas on all subjects. The one thing they all have in common is that they are highly regarded films that have received critical acclaim from all over. Ticket prices vary, but in general have gotten quite high in the past few years. If you decide that this is the kind of entertainment you could handle often, then join the "Friends Of Film." For $50 a year you get about ten different tickets and the Film Calendar mailed to you, along with all sorts of special privileges. You can also get a Film Scrip (six admission tickets) for $30, or $25 for MFA members and students. This is no saving, but it's a great motivation to get you out to see some of the MFA's otherwise hard-to-find films in this excellent theater.

If the admission is still too rich for your blood, then you and your date could become *Volunteer Ushers*. Sound silly? It's a great way to see all the films you can handle without paying a dime or having to wear polyester uniforms. The work is just handing out a few programs and then you enjoy watching the movie for free.

Remember: Any date who doesn't respect your appreciation of the free things in life isn't worth your time—or your dime.

ADDRESS 465 Huntington Avenue, Fenway.

PHONE 267-9300, ext. 300 (ext. 306 for Volunteer Usher information).

PRICES Usually $6–8, or *FREE* for Volunteer Ushers (see above).

DIRECTIONS The MFA is located on Huntington Avenue across from Northeastern University.

By T: Take the Green Line E train to the Ruggles/Museum stop. The MFA is across the street.

PARKING Most films are shown at night when there is ample and *FREE* parking on the street.

BRATTLE THEATER

The Brattle is so Cambridge.

What is Cambridge, you ask?

Good question. It's hard to tell these days whether Cambridge is a teenage, black clothes, body-piercing mecca or the intellectual hotbed of old.

Opinions vary, and one of the best places to form your own is the Brattle Theater where Cantabrigians (that really is the word—I looked it up) have been going for theater enjoyment for over 100 years. When going to the Brattle, you can expect anything from foreign and independent films to classical movies, but you can count on quality movies that you won't get just anywhere.

Despite having experienced a recent price increase, jacking the admission from $6 to $6.75, I still think we can call it a Cheap Date—especially considering the double feature deal. Just about every night of the week (as long as they aren't showing the same movie all night) you can get into two showings for only $6.75. Also, if you only want to see the last show, you can get in for just $6 (still better than your local moviedrome).

Another bargain is the 6 discount tickets for only $30. By purchasing these you will not only get tickets at the low price of $5 each, but you will have future encouragement to go back to the Brattle. If you become a member of the Brattle Theater for $50 a year, then you can get into all the shows for only $4.

To find out what is playing you can call their recorded line at 876-6837, or you can pick up one of their two-month schedules (strongly recommended) so you and your date can plan ahead to catch that favorite unfindable-even-on-video classic.

While you're at the Brattle Theater, you absolutely have to try out Cafe Algiers, upstairs from the theater. If this incensed Eastern-style cafe is not to your liking, there are plenty of other coffeehouses in the area to explore like Passim (around the corner off of Church Street on Palmer Street) or Nameless Coffeehouse (in the basement of the First Parish Church on Church Street near Mass. Ave.). A stop at one of these spots afterward should help you answer the question, What is Cambridge?

ADDRESS 40 Brattle Street, Harvard Square.

PHONE 876-6837 (recordings), 876-6838 (a person).

PRICES Tickets for double features: $6.75 and $6 for first matinee and last show; $4 at all times for children and seniors.

DIRECTIONS Brattle Street sprouts off curvy Eliot Street right at HMV Records in the heart of Harvard Square. If you're at a loss, anyone can point it out to you.

By T: Since it's only a block from the Harvard Square T station, the T is a smart option. From the exit at Out of Town Ticket Agency, cross Mass. Ave. toward the Out of Town newspaper stand and follow the sidewalk of shops (musicians, students, freaks, et al) around the bend till you're across the street from the theater.

PARKING If you dare to drive, the Brattle Theater offers discount parking behind the theater at University Place Parking Garage, located at 124 Mt. Auburn Street.

CINE CLUB AT THE FRENCH LIBRARY

One of the best spots in Boston to enjoy a good foreign film is the Cine Club at the French Library.

Oh great! Ancient French films with elaborate plots involving annoying mimes, you say.

But you are misinformed. Although you may encounter a mime from time to time, it's not the norm. All of the evening films are subtitled, so you can leave your French dictionaries at home. Most of these movies were recently in the theaters, some are classics and all of them are excellent.

The cozy viewing room is actually an ornate hall of the French Library, well equipped with a giant movie screen, sufficiently comfortable chairs and an excellent date atmosphere. Admission is only $5 for non-members ($4 for members), and you can get a set of ten passes for $35—that's right, a $15 saving! Wednesdays they show *FREE* movies at 1:30 p.m.

Call the French Library to see what's playing and to be put on the mailing list.

ADDRESS 53 Marlborough Street, Back Bay.

PHONE 266-4351.

HOURS Movies usually begin at 8. Call ahead.

PRICES For non-members $5 ($4 for members).

DIRECTIONS The French Library is on Marlborough Street at the corner of Berkeley Street, one block from the Public Garden.

By T: Take the Green Line to the Arlington Street stop. Walk down Arlington Street past the Public Garden until Marlborough Street. Take a left onto Marlborough Street and walk one block to find the French Library on the right corner of Berkeley Street.

PARKING There are usually parking spots available on Marlborough Street or Berkeley Street. It can be difficult to find spots in prime day hours. Bring quarters.

HARVARD FILM ARCHIVE

Aren't you tired of going to movie theaters where you miss half the lines because people are talking incessantly? This won't happen at the Harvard Film Archive (HFA) series at the Carpenter Center for Visual Arts: The HFA boasts having ejection seats for those constant chatterboxes. The cozy and extra-comfortable theater isn't even the best part of the HFA. What really makes it stand above your average movie complex is the selection of films. From fine art films to wild, fast paced flicks, the HFA has got it and they flaunt it for a mere $6 ($5 for students). They have films every night of the week and usually have about three showings of all varieties nightly.

While you're there, it is unheard of to leave the Carpenter Center without checking out some of the displays of visual arts. The center also hosts many lectures that shouldn't be missed. In fact, it is impossible to ever visit the Carpenter Center without having much to discuss with your date.

To get a complete listing of all the activities going on with the HFA and throughout the Carpenter Center, pick up a two-month schedule at their lobby or call them and ask what's happening. And don't worry, you don't have to be a Harvard legacy to be admitted.

ADDRESS 24 Quincy Street, Harvard Square.

PHONE 495-3251.

HOURS Movies times change; call ahead for the schedule.

PRICES $6 for adults and $5 for students; $60 for a series of 15 films.

DIRECTIONS The Carpenter Center for Visual Arts is located on Quincy Street across from Harvard Yard and next to the Fogg Art Museum.

By T: From the Harvard Square stop on the Red Line take a right onto Mass. Ave., then a left onto Quincy Street. The HFA is up the block on the right, before the Fogg.

PARKING Parking is a bit easier at night and usually available on Quincy Street or surrounding streets.

WANG CENTER CLASSIC FILM SERIES

This one goes in the too-good-to-be-true category. Not only does the Wang Center show some of the greatest movies of all time, but they show them in the beautifully restored Wang Center! I can't think of any place in Boston that is quite as beautiful as the Wang. But this gets even better.

The series, which has just been revived, shows fantastic films like *Gone With The Wind*, *The Godfather*, *Ben Hur*, and other classics for only $6. At this time, the series only runs from January through April. But it's a great way to brighten up those dreary winter months. The films are shown every other Monday and all shows start at 7 p.m. Tickets can be purchased at the box office, or by calling Ticketmaster at 931-2000.

Don't let this season pass by without taking advantage of this great opportunity to see classic films in Boston's most beautiful theater.

ADDRESS 270 Tremont Street, Theater District.

PHONE Wang Center: 482-9393 Ticket Master 931-2000.

PRICES Prices vary, but are usually around $6.

DIRECTIONS The Wang Center is in the heart of the Theater District near the intersection of Stuart Street.

By T: Take the Green Line to the Boylston Street station, then walk about two blocks toward the Theater District to find the Wang Center on your left side.

PARKING Parking in the Theater District is usually awful, but since this will be on a Monday before 7 p.m., you should be able to find a convenient street spot.

FREE FRIDAY FLICKS AT THE ESPLANADE
June through August

Free Friday Flicks are one of Boston's most wonderful offerings for summertime dating. It's outdoors at the Hatch Shell, in a beautiful spot with the Charles River in the background . . . and it's *FREE*! Need I say more? The series usually begins around the third Friday of June and runs through Labor Day. Schedules can be obtained from the Hatch Shell during the movies or by mail from the Metropolitan District Commission (MDC). Since nothing in Boston is ever certain, make sure you know there is a movie going on this Friday before you trot on down; they occasionally skip a Friday. Your best bet for confirmation is to call the MDC at 727-9548 for all the vital information.

Movies begin at 8:30, but try to arrive early enough to sit up close. If you're not close enough, the acoustics can get a little fuzzy with the din of Storrow Drive. If you pack a picnic dinner, a blanket and those little folding beach chairs that are always a success, you've got all the makings of a perfect evening. An ice cream cone at one of Charles Street's creameries might be a grand finale to your romantic evening under the stars.

ADDRESS Esplanade, Boston.

PHONE MDC: 727-9548.

HOURS Movies begin Fridays at 8:30.

The series runs from late June to mid-September. Make sure to confirm first. For a schedule of movies send a stamped self-addressed envelope to:

MDC
20 Somerset Street, 4th Floor
Boston, MA 02108

PRICES *FREE*

DIRECTIONS At Beacon and Arlington streets, cross the orange-pink Fiedler Footbridge to find the Hatch Shell facing you on the Esplanade.

By T: Take the Green Line to the Arlington Street stop. Walk down Arlington Street toward the Charles River. At the end of Arlington Street walk over the orange-pink bridge to the Esplanade.

PARKING It's definitely difficult to park here. Make sure to go very early so you don't miss any of the film. Try Beacon Street and other surrounding streets.

BOSTON PUBLIC LIBRARY FILM SERIES

Want to see a good movie in a killer theater? If you do, go to the Boston Public Library (BPL).

Oh, great. a public library movie. The last thing I want to do with a date is see a movie about the reproductive habits of mosquitoes on the Nile!

WRONG! How do *Harold and Maude, Funny Girl, It's a Wonderful Life* and other totally normal Hollywood movies sound? The BPL runs retrospectives of actors, directors and other important people while also showing docudramas, animations and other movies that will entertain almost any crowd.

Another big plus about the BPL is their auditorium. The films are shown in the Rabb Lecture Hall where the climate is controlled; it's amazingly comfortable and it's got fantastic acoustics. The BPL manages to show about four movies a week, usually quite different. Call the BPL and ask what movie they're showing this week, or stop by and pick up a schedule. You can usually get one at any branch. Also, most of the other BPL branches show their own film series. The auditoriums aren't as good, but the movies are just as entertaining and just as *FREE*.

ADDRESS 666 Boylston Street, Copley Square.

PHONE 536-5400. Call and ask what films are on this week.

HOURS Movies are one night a week and usually start at 6 p.m., but call to confirm.

PRICES *FREE*

DIRECTIONS See page 187 for directions.

PARKING See page 187 for parking hints.

More good cinemas:

    COOLIDGE CORNER CINEMA 290 Harvard Street, Brookline 734-2500.

    BOSTON VIDEO AND FILM FOUNDATION 1126 Boylston Street, Suite 201, Boston 536-1540

    HARVARD-EPWORTH SERIES 1555 Mass. Ave., Harvard Square 354-0837.

    INSTITUTE OF CONTEMPORARY ART 955 Boylston Street, Boston 266-5152.

    OMNI THEATER at Science Museum, Science Park, Boston 723-2500.

COLLEGE PERFORMANCES

It would be criminal to live in Boston and put up with the disadvantages of a college town without reaping the many benefits. If you haven't already discovered the fountain of resources that academia can be, the following would be a good place to start. These schools work long and hard to put on quality shows, and admission is usually a steal. Each school provides an easy way to find out about their performances using your phone, getting a mailing or both! Once you've seen what's out there, you'll never pay top dollar for a performance again.

BOSTON UNIVERSITY (BU)

    Even if I weren't a BU graduate, I would have to give this university very high marks (higher than the marks they ever gave me) for providing an inordinate amount of events for their students and for the general public. Did I mention that tons of these events (and I mean good events) are *FREE*? So I try never to miss any of these *FREE* offerings. In fact I try to get everyone I know—BU alum or not—to come to all of BU's *FREE* activities. I guess it's my way of making those tuition dollars stretch a long, long way.

But even if you didn't spend any money at BU on tuition, you'll be doing yourself a favor by attending some of their outstanding performances.

BU has several performance halls and a slew of different troupes that guarantee a wide variety of fine entertainment. BU also has a Nexus bulletin board telephone system that allows you to receive recorded information about performances, ticket prices and locations. Call 353-4000, then press 2 to get into the Nexus system and 215 (216 for music performances) for their latest performing arts offerings.

Ticket prices range from *FREE* to $10 at the most. Most shows take place at the BU-tiful Tsai Center on the BU campus.

Many of their performances are at different locations, so make sure you know where you're going. If you want to talk to a real person about these things call 353-3345. And remember, you can't spell BUdget without BU!

ADDRESS Tsai Center, 685 Commonwealth Avenue, Boston. Other events take place at other locations, so make sure you know where you're going!

PHONE 353-4000. Press 2 to get into Nexus and then 215 for theater, 216 for music performances. Call 353-3329 for the art gallery shows and lectures. If you want to talk to a real person, call 353-3345 during business hours.

PRICES From *FREE* to about $10.

DIRECTIONS The Tsai Center is located on Commonwealth Avenue at the heart of BU, about three blocks from Kenmore Square.

By T: Take Green Line B train to BU Central. When you get off you are standing in front of the Tsai Center.

PARKING There is meter parking all along Commonwealth Avenue and side streets.

MASSACHUSETTS INSTITUTE OF TECHNOLOGY (MIT)

If you have a phone near you, pick it up and dial 253-ARTS. I'm waiting! Really, do it!

Now, aren't you amazed at the abundance of performances, efficiency of information and *FREE* or very low prices? I bet you'd agree that MIT's name should be MIEE: Massachusetts Institute of Economical Entertainment. Not only do they put on tons of shows, concerts and events, but they make it all as easy as possible to find out what's happening. Most of MIT's performances are *FREE* or under $5. The music department alone has about seven different performance groups, and it hosts many visiting guests from Boston and around the world.

Despite MIT not being a performance school, they manage to have weekly series of performances. Thursdays at noon are Chapel Concert Series; Fridays at noon are part of the Advanced Music Performance Student Recitals at Killian Hall; Saturday concerts at 8 p.m. are more of a grab bag of performances, with the student Concert Band performing some weeks and the Guest Artists series others. Some of MIT's best shows and events happen at the end of the each term when all the student groups put on their finest shows, concerts, plays and exhibits. You name it, MIT's got it.

There are many ways to find out about MIT's plethora of performances. You can call the Art Hotline (253-ARTS) for most events, or call their Concert Hotline at 253-9800. Since MIT has an overwhelming amount of possibilities, it may be smart to get your hands on a calendar of each semester's events. They will gladly put you on their mailing list if you call them and then you will always know what the geniuses . . . or is it genii . . . at MIT have in store for you.

Performances take place at different locations around campus, so make sure you know which one is where. To round out your

MIT experience, try a meal, or just a drink, at The Miracle of Science (321 Mass. Ave.) where cheap food and drink are as abundant as hydrogen in the sun.

ADDRESS 77 Mass. Ave., Cambridge.

Shows take place at a variety of locations. A few are:
> MIT Chapel opposite 77 Mass. Ave..
> Kresge Auditorium 84 Mass. Ave.
> Killian Hall 60 Memorial Drive, room 14W-111.

PHONE Art Hotline 253-ARTS (2787); Concert Hotline: 253-9800; Arts Office (for a person) 253-4003.

PRICES Most performances are *FREE* or less than $5.

DIRECTIONS The MIT Chapel is just past the MIT bridge on the left side of Mass. Ave., across the street from the huge main MIT building at 77 Mass. Ave.

Kresge Auditorium is off Amherst Street (first left after the MIT Bridge toward the Museum of Science). From Amherst Street, the copper-domed Kresge Auditorium will be on your right side and the parking lot directly in front of you.

Killian Hall is on Memorial Drive, east of Mass. Ave. just past the large Killian Courtyard.

By T: MIT has its own T stop, Kendall, on the Red Line (toward Alewife from Park Street). The exit is at Main Street on the east side of campus. Everyone at MIT is very friendly and helpful, so just ask directions to your destination.

PARKING MIT provides *FREE* parking for concerts at night and on weekends. For Kresge Auditorium and MIT Chapel concerts, park at the Kresge Parking Lot on Amherst Street next to the auditorium.

There is *FREE* parking for Killian Hall concerts at the East Parking Lot on the corner of Vassar and Main streets, but this is quite a distance from Killian Hall, and you are better off looking for parking along Memorial Drive.

LONGY SCHOOL OF MUSIC

Located in always hip Harvard Square, the Longy School (pronounced lon-jee) is one of the best sources for *FREE* or insanely inexpensive musical entertainment. Besides having terrific performances of every kind of music for *FREE* (or sometimes about $5–15), the Longy School makes it soooo easy to find out what's going on. The music varies greatly, from experimental to innovative traditional. There is truly something for everybody. But don't take my word for it, call for yourself.

There are two simple ways to find out about their events: one is to call their events line at 876-0956. Make sure to have a pen and paper handy because Longy has tons of events every week. The second way to get information, and somewhat easier on the ears, is to be put on their mailing list (call same number, ext. 120). They will promptly send you a calendar that has something to offer about 28 nights of the month. Most of their events take place at 27 Garden Street, except for the occasional performance at the awe-inspiring Jordan Hall. A terrific incentive to go on weeknights is that there is *FREE* validated parking at the Everett Street Garage. Otherwise, the cheapest and easiest way to get there is to take the T.

ADDRESS Performances take place at 27 Garden Street, Harvard Square.

PHONE 876-0956 (ext. 991 for events and ext. 120 for mailing list).

PRICES Tickets are often *FREE*. Otherwise they run $5–15.

DIRECTIONS Enter Harvard Square from Memorial Drive via JFK Boulevard, pass the information booth on the right (The Coop on the left), pass the Garden Street light and make a U-turn around the median. Then turn right onto Garden Street. The school is three blocks up just past the Sheraton Commander Hotel. For directions to Jordan Hall see page 70.

By T: Take the Red Line to Harvard Square and exit at the Church Street exit. Once aboveground, take a left onto Garden Street just past First Parish Church. Follow Garden Street for three blocks and the school is about a half a block from the Sheraton Commander Hotel.

PARKING Other than always-frustrating on-street parking in Harvard Square, there is free validated parking on weeknights at the Everett Street Garage. Call for details.

BERKLEE COLLEGE OF MUSIC AT
BERKLEE PERFORMANCE CENTER

The Berklee Performance Center is host to many big shows including comedy, rock, jazz and classical music performances. The only drawback is that tickets for these shows are the usual $20–25 prices—you'd think if they charged that much they could afford to get rid of the rainbow on the façade of their concert hall!

Anyway, a better bargain is to attend the Berklee School of Music's Student/Faculty Concert Series. For the oh-so-low price of $1–4, you can see these well-regarded and often ingenious performances in their state-of-the-art concert hall.

You can find out about Berklee School of Music performances with the touch of your finger by calling their concert line at 266-7455. The concert line will give you information on their mainline shows and then tell you of the performances with considerably cheaper ticket prices.

For cheap fare, try Cafe Jaffa at 48 Gloucester Street. It's got great, inexpensive Middle Eastern food and Turkish coffee to get you geared up for the performance.

ADDRESS 136 Mass. Ave., Back Bay.

PHONE Concert line: 266-7455. Offices: 266-1400.

PRICES Ticket prices for the student/faculty shows are $4–7.

DIRECTIONS The Berklee Performance Center is easy to find, on the corner of Mass. Ave. and Boylston Street near Tower Records.

By T: The Hynes Convention Center/Auditorium station on the Green Line is one block away from Berklee, underneath Tower Records.

PARKING This is one of the more difficult places to park, but at night one can often find spots on Mass. Ave. down by the Christian Science Church (near Westland Avenue), or on Boylston Street where the Turnpike rumbles below.

NEW ENGLAND CONSERVATORY at JORDAN HALL

The New England Conservatory (NEC), being the oldest music school in the country, is also one of the greatest contributors of cultural entertainment in this grand city of ours.

Just about every night of the week you can saunter down to the NEC and see a *FREE* concert. But if that isn't enough or if you're picturing sitting in on a classroom recital, keep reading! Just going to the NEC's Jordan Hall alone is truly worth the visit. Even if you're dating someone with no interest in classical music, it will still be worth the effort to get him or her to Jordan Hall. This beautiful and acoustically exceptional concert hall will tug at anyone's heartstrings. Trust me: when the notes soar, so will your relationship.

The other wonderful thing about the NEC's *FREE* concerts is the audience. If you like to hear music but don't want to put on your Sunday best, you don't have to. The audience is made up of 80 percent students who dress just as they please. But on the other hand, if you feel like donning some slick duds for the evening, you will be perfectly at home. The student populated audience is also surprisingly polite—because most of them are performers themselves, they know exactly how to behave. Honestly, you won't find a better audience at the most expensive symphonies.

Most of the *FREE* NEC concerts are held at Jordan Hall, especially those during the week, and it is always a treat to hear any kind of music in this lovely golden hall. When Jordan Hall is booked for those hoity toity, high-priced concerts we want to avoid, the *FREE* concerts are held in the smaller and a bit less elegant William and Brown hall. No matter where you hear the notes played, there is no denying that the maestros at NEC put on a beautiful concert for a price that can't be matched.

The NEC has a concert line (262-1120, ext. 700) for information out about all the performances. Pick up a calendar at any time from the front hall of Jordan Hall. If you want a calendar sent to your home call 262-1120, ext. 420. They may ask you for a donation; you need only give as little as $5 for a year of the calendar.

ADDRESS Jordan Hall and William Hall 30 Gainsborough Street.

PHONE Concert line: 262-1120, ext. 700.
Offices: 262-1120, ext. 420.

PRICES Most concerts are *FREE* unless otherwise noted.

DIRECTIONS Jordan Hall and the NEC are located at the corner of Huntington and Gainsborough streets, one block west of Symphony Hall.

By T: The closest T stop is Symphony Hall on the Green Line. From the exit, walk to Huntington Avenue, take a right and then a left onto Gainsborough Street. Another close T stop is Mass. Ave. on the Orange Line. From here, walk to Huntington Avenue, take a left and then a right onto Gainsborough Street.

PARKING There is parking available at an adjacent parking garage, or on the streets surrounding Jordan Hall including Saint Botolph Street, Huntington Avenue and Gainsborough Street.

BOSTON CONSERVATORY

I always hear people say that Boston is a black hole of dance performance. I used to agree, but once a little research was done, I realized that Boston is only a black hole of expensive dance performance. So, without blowing a wad on tickets to the Boston Ballet, you could visit the Boston Conservatory for a close second in the ballet department.

As for the rest of their performances, they are all equally exciting. The Boston Conservatory features performances including plays, orchestral works, dance recitals and concerts galore. To hear a recording of the latest schedule call 536-3063. They will tell you what's on, when and where. Most performances take place in one of four places: The Boston Conservatory Theater, Suelly Hall, St. Cecilia's Church (orchestra events) or at The First and Second Church (yes, that's one place). As a general rule, tickets are $10 per person and $7 for students. But many of their programs are *FREE*, especially the musical performances. Just call the main number to find out which ones are *FREE*, and then go. You've nothing to lose. Most of their performance halls are very accommodating and quite comfortable.

ADDRESS 8 The Fenway, Boston.

Performances are at:

> Suelly Hall, 8 The Fenway, across from the Fens near Boylston Street
>
> The Boston Conservatory Theater, 33 Hemenway Street is one block up Boylston Street towards Mass. Ave.; take a right and the theater will be on the right side.
>
> First and Second Church, 66 Marlborough Street at the corner of Berkeley Street.
>
> St. Cecilia's Church, 30 Cecilia's Street off Mass. Ave. next to the Berklee School of Music.

PHONE 536-3063 (recording of events); 536-6340 (Box Office).

HOURS The Box Office is open Mon–Fri 9–6 (but hours vary).

PRICES Very often *FREE*, but if not $10–15 ($7–10 for students). Call Box Office.

EMERSON COLLEGE

How does a stroll through the Public Garden, maybe a ride on the swan boats, or a picnic and then a show at Emerson College sound to you?

Expensive, you say?

Pshaw!

Emerson College is a great source of fine entertainment for little dough. And since Emerson College is in the heart of Boston near the Public Garden, it is accessible to just about anyone.

Emerson manages to put out quite a few performances each season. These include dance groups, comedy, dramas, spring musicals, film screenings and an annual Emerson College playwright's festival. To get on the mailing list of these upcoming events call the Performing Arts Center at 578-8780. If you want to find out what is going on now, call the Box Office at 578-8785. The Box Office is open weekdays 12–4 and although it is closed during school vacations, you can always hear a recording of upcoming events. Ticket prices run the gamut from *FREE* to about $20 at the most. Okay, I'll admit the $20 shows are overpriced, so only go to the *FREE* or under $10 ones! Students always get a discount, so don't forget your college ID. Be warned that Emerson College doesn't always perform on its own turf; make sure to know exactly where the show is. Sometimes they perform at some real snazzy joints!

ADDRESS 100 Beacon Street, Boston.

PHONE Performing Arts Center 578-8780; Box Office (recording when closed) 578-8785.

HOURS The Box Office is open noon–4.

PRICES From *FREE* to $20.

NORTHEASTERN

Did you think that all Northeastern had to offer was some Division III sporting events? If so, luckily you were wrong. They've got a ton of stuff for young poor folk like me.

Each year Northeastern puts out a program called nuArts. In it you can find a complete list of all of their impressive special guest performances. These performances are *FREE* for students and well-priced for the rest of us. Northeastern also has a bunch of other performances from music to athletics. These ticket prices vary, but you can usually plan on spending about $5. Call and they'll put you on the mailing list, or if you can't wait for the US Postal Service, call their Box Office and ask what's coming up. As Northeastern is vast and traverses Boston, make sure you know exactly where you are headed.

Yes, you can also check out their sporting events.

ADDRESS 360 Huntington Avenue, Boston.

PHONE 373-2247.

PRICES Most performances are *FREE* for students, and about $5 for everyone else.

HARVARD

It would be negligent to do a section on college offerings without including Harvard University, across the river. From lectures to experimental theater, Harvard abounds in opportunities. The best way to get information on all events is to call the activities office at 495-1718. It's a long recorded message, but you can skip any section of the message by pressing 33 from a touch-tone phone. Or, pick up a copy of the *Harvard Gazette* (listing a two-week schedule of programs) at the Harvard Information Office in Holyoke Center on Harvard Square.

Although performances happen all over Cambridge and elsewhere, the best ones take place at Loeb Theater (see American Repertory Theater, pg. 18), Agassiz Center and the magnificent

Sanders Theater at the newly-restored Memorial Hall—a Gothic wonder by itself. Most lectures are *FREE* and usually offer refreshments, while tickets to performances run $5–18 with special rates for students.

Sanders Theater also has many independent performances of music, comedians and just about anything. Although these are often a bit pricey ($12–22), they are well-priced for professional performances. Call 496-2222 for the complete recording of events.

ADDRESS Sanders Theater in Memorial Hall at corner of Quincy and Cambridge streets across from the fire station in Harvard Square. Agassiz Center at 64 Brattle in Radcliffe Yard, is across from the Loeb Drama Center.
Loeb Drama Center: See American Repertory Theater.

PHONE Recorded events: 495-1718; press 33 to skip forward.

HOURS The Box Office is open 12–6, seven days a week.

PRICES Many events are *FREE*; others are $5–18 with special discounts for students.

Other college offerings:

    BOSTON COLLEGE 140 Commonwealth Avenue, Chestnut Hill 552-4800.

    BRANDEIS 415 South Street, Waltham 736-4300.

    NEW SCHOOL OF MUSIC 25 Lowell Street, Cambridge 492-8105.

    PINE MANOR COLLEGE 400 Heath Street, Chestnut Hill 731-7118.

    TUFTS UNIVERSITY College Avenue, Medford 627-3493.

ART GALLERIES

!ATTENTION FOAG VICTIMS!

Are you uncomfortable going into an art gallery that doesn't charge an entrance fee because you feel you have to have a special invitation?

Frightened that gallery people will slap your wrists or shun you for wearing sneakers?

If you've answered yes to either of these, you must be suffering from Fear Of Art Galleries, or FOAG as it is called by professional FOAG counselors. The FOAG complex is common among young adults. In fact, I too once suffered from FOAG symptoms. I've undergone all possible therapy, and the one that worked the best was this: *JUST DO IT!* (I know you probably thought Nike Shoes came up with that saying, but they really got it from the FOAG Club motto.)

Here's what you do: below are listed a few of the galleries on Boston's premiere gallery concourse, Newbury Street. Once you've catapulted yourself into a few of these galleries, you'll gain much confidence and before you know it you will be through with FOAG. Soon you'll be popping into galleries all over town—even looking under "galleries" in the Yellow Pages to somehow satiate your desire for *FREE ART*!

Here's a tip: there's nothing more luxurious than alternating your gallery visits with cappuccino and pastry stops. Newbury Street happens to be particularly good for this kind of indulgence. So go ahead, treat yourself.

NEWBURY STREET GALLERIES
Note: The # is the street number on Newbury Street.

#8 - *Vincent's Obsession Works of Art* Believe it or not, the name is not the best part of this gallery. The exhibits change frequently, but always provide a fascinating array of art forms with a concentration on Latin American artists. 424-8888. Tue–Sat 10–6.

#29 - *Newbury Fine Arts* What uniqueness the name does not have is made up for in their presentation of chic modern art with a southwestern influence. 536-0210. Mon–Wed and Fri 10–6, Sun 12–5.

#32 - *Bronte Contemporary Arts* Indeed contemporary, Yankel Ginzbury utilizes all mediums with his art. Some interesting sculptures. 236-1303. Mon–Sat 11–6, Sun 12–5.

#39 - *Mann Gallery* This doll infested salon has some of the most beautiful barbies in town (okay, they're not barbies). I never knew that dolls could be so interesting (and expensive). Try it out. 266-MANN. Wed–Fri 9-6, Sat 12–5 (if it's nice out).

#77 - *Arvest Gallery* On the second floor, the Arvest Gallery displays more classical art than many of its neighbors, with a concentration of American 19th-century art.

#81 - *Brenda Taylor Gallery* One of the more professional looking galleries on the block, Brenda Taylor Gallery consistently displays quality art work of museum caliber. 859-7677. Mon–Sat 10–6.

#122 - *Nathalie Tschudin* Ms. Tschudin's objective has been to give smaller European artists a chance to exhibit their work in America. This large two-room gallery usually exhibits three up-and-coming artists who have never before been viewed here.

#123 - *Randal Beck* Randal Beck has a more industrial style of art. The paintings look a bit sparse, but they inspire some diverse conversations. 266-2475. Tues-Sat 10–5.

#129 - *Arden Gallery* The bright Arden Gallery displays funky modern art of all different mediums. Arden has some mesmerizing wall hangings. 247-0610. Tues-Sat 11–5.

#158 - *The Copley Society of Boston* The Copley Society of Boston probably has the most thorough collection of local artistry. You can get some cool invites, too! 536-5049. Tues–Sat 10:30–5:30.

#158 - *Alfred J. Walker* A quaint second-floor apartment is home to this random collection of classical paintings. Display is not the primary intention here, and many paintings are just leaned up against the wall in stacks. But don't be fooled, there is more to see here than at many of the more pretentious-looking galleries. 247-1319. Tues–Sat 10–5.

#162 - *Guild of Boston Artists* The Guild is probably the most museum-like gallery on the street. One can find a wide variety of paintings from the area's finest artists along with chairs and couches to sit and ponder the art; just like a museum, but no fee! 536-7660. Tues–Sat 10–5.

#169 - *Childs Gallery* This dark and ominous establishment is the quintessential art gallery. Ring the bell to get in and you will find two floors of magnificent oil paintings, large and small. But the unique yet classical sculptures are what set this gallery apart. 266-1108. Tues–Fri 9–6, Mon–Sat 10–5.

#171 - *Pucker Gallery* Pucker Gallery has a tremendous amount to offer any viewer, from large sculptures to small trinket art; not to mention the paintings. If you feel really inspired by this place, then ask to see their Modern Masters collection including Picasso, Chagall and Matisse. *AMAZING!* 267-9473. Mon–Sat 10–5:30, Sun 1–5.

#173 - *Chase Gallery* One of Boston's most acclaimed galleries, Chase Gallery offers different exhibits monthly, with a consistent array of mediums and styles. 859-7222. Mon–Sat 10–6, Sun 1–5.

#179 - *Nielsen Gallery* The different rooms at Nielsen Gallery are always sure to offer you a wild variety of art. Exhibits rotate and they are usually quite contemporary. 266-4835. Tues–Sat 10–5:30.

#205 - *Newman Gallery* Another museum-like gallery that tends to have large works, exquisitely arranged. Here both atmosphere and quality reign. 262-9083. Tue–Sat 10–5, Sun 12–5.

#324 - *Nostalgia Factory* Okay. It's not really a gallery, but it is a great way to round off your tour of Newbury Street. It's a pop art haven filled with visuals that will take you back to your childhood and unlock all those old memories. One of the few places where the name does exemplify the contents. 236-8754. Mon–Thur 10–7, Fri–Sat 10–8, Sun 11–7.

Some more great galleries:

    88 ROOM 107 Brighton Avenue, Allston 562-0840.

    ALON GALLERY 1665A Beacon Street, Brookline 232-3388.

    BROMFIELD GALLERY 90 South Street, Boston 451-5995.

    CAMBRIDGE ART ASSOCIATION 25 Lowell Street, Cambridge 876-0246.

    CHAPEL GALLERY 60 Highland Street, Newton 244-4039.

    GENOVESE GALLERY 535 Albany Street, Boston 426-9738.

    PIANO FACTORY GALLERY 791 Tremont Street, Boston 437-9365.

    SIGNATURE & GROHE GLASS GALLERY 24 North Dock Square, North End 227-4885.

FEASTING BOSTON

EATING OUT

Many people consider eating out a major source of entertainment. And I agree that a special meal out at a restaurant is ideal. But to go to a restaurant and hurriedly scarf down a meal so that you can get to the theater on time is a waste of money. If you're going to go out to eat, it should be the main focus of your date. For the most part, trying to jam in too many events in one date is not only costly, but often a real hassle.

In reading the entries below, you may ask yourself what criteria have been used to select these spots. Although a few of the entries are more inexpensive than romantic, the ideal restaurant combines tasty and modestly priced food with a romantic atmosphere. Anyone can find cheap food, but finding it in a restaurant where you're proud to bring a date is the challenge. Hopefully the entries below include something for everyone — be it Italian, fancy, diner or vegetarian food. Let these restaurants be just the beginning of your quest for the perfect restaurant date.

A NOTE ON PRICES

One of the annoying things about writing restaurant reviews is that prices, menus and other important details often change. Each entry has a general price range given for appetizers, dinners and drinks, to be used as a measuring stick to see if this restaurant is in your budget. Individual prices (when given) are rounded off to save space. In the event that a menu has changed, I apologize for being outdated and hope the new menu is not too different from the old.

TWO WAYS TO KEEP RESTAURANT CHECKS LOW
(No—not tipping the waiter is not an option. But it is a double negative.)

1) "A Cheap Date is one that doesn't drink" my Grandmother always says, "But so is a boring one," I would usually respond. It's true, alcohol can really weigh down an entertainment budget. But there is a way that you can have your punch and drink it too. Many of Boston's cheaper (and often newer) restaurants that don't yet have their liquor license will allow you to Bring Your Own Booze. Just call ahead and ask if they have a license and if you can BYOB.

2) Most people find that they usually can't finish a whole meal at a restaurant. If you don't order an entrée and just get an appetizer or two or a side dish, you can save tons of money and still get about the same amount of food. Or if you and your date have similar tastes, you can split and appetizer and an entrée. So next time you want to eat out but not pig out, keep in mind which restaurants

serve particularly large portions and then go halfsies or just get an appetizer. (Some restaurants will charge extra for splitting orders, but they will say so on the menu—and chances are it will still qualify as a Cheap Date.)

IRUÑA

A small, sweet Spanish restaurant tucked into the busy life of Harvard Square, Iruña does some exciting things with Spanish specialties. My favorites are Paella (pronounced pie-ay-yah) ($11); the Carneguis Adea (pronounced carn-ee-juis) ($9), which is chunks of beef in a carrot and white wine sauce; and the Pork Tenderloin (pronounced oink-er-icius) ($9) with a wonderful mushroom and white wine sauce with steamed artichokes. There are also a variety of omelets and other Spanish specialties, and all entrées include soup and salad. If you want to add some potency to your date, you must have the sangria; a whole pitcher is only $7 and will add a little blush to anyone's cheeks. Beers are quite reasonable at $3, as is the house wine. In general, I find Iruña to be very generous with their portions . . . it's a Spanish thing.

During the summer months, you can sit outside on the back patio, giving the effect of being in someone's backyard—and in Cambridge, you probably are. Indoors, too, is softly lit and romantic, especially on a cold winter's night. Iruña is a nice change from the usual fast-pace, eat and run restaurant. Visit Iruña when you have time to savor the fine flavors and enjoy this peaceful oasis.

ADDRESS 56 JFK Boulevard, Harvard Square.

PHONE 868-5633.

HOURS Mon–Thur 11–2 and 6–9; Fri–Sun 11:30–10. *CLOSED SUNDAYS*. Hours vary with the seasons. Call ahead.

PRICES Appetizers: $2–5; Entrées: $7–15; Drinks: $3–$5 a glass.

DIRECTIONS Although Iruña is right on JFK Boulevard, it is somewhat tucked back. It's directly across the street from the Janus Theater.

By T: From the Harvard Square station on the Red Line, take a left onto JFK Boulevard and walk toward the river. Iruña will be in the second block on the left.

PARKING It's always the catch in Harvard Square, but you can try parking on Memorial Drive (read the parking signs carefully). It's not a far walk from Iruña.

GRENDEL'S BAR

I wasn't the biggest fan of Grendel's Den until I learned about their Happy Hour deal downstairs at Grendel's Bar. Now, you'll find me there about three times a week! Every weekday (Sunday–Thursday 5–7 and 9:30–11; and Friday 5–7) you can have any appetizer at the bar for $1.50. You're probably thinking, "Oh great, a bag of pork rinds for a buck fifty!" But I mean some serious appetizers. In fact, I mean *DINNER for $1.50*!

They have enormous sandwiches stuffed with meats and goodies of all kinds, popcorn shrimp, humus and tahini, Snake Eggs (don't get sick—it's cheese and jalapeno rice fritters), French bread pizza, cala-can-you-believe-it-mari, buffalo wings, nachos, quesadillas, steamed artichokes, chickenfingers and did I mention *BURGERS*? And yes, its only $1.50.

The only catch is that you have to order alcohol—twist my arm. Expecting that drink prices are out of this world? Wrong again! All beers, including an extensive collection of draught and bottled beers, are only $2.65–3.50. All other drinks are reasonable too (wine can be a little pricey).

The bar itself is quite spacious and has an almost intellectual atmosphere. There's a huge fireplace that roars in winter. There are plenty of tables that become a hot commodity as the night progresses.

The best advice I can give you is try to get there early when it's easy to get the waitresses' attention and nothing is sold out. Trust me, people take advantage of this opportunity, so you've got to get there and claim what's rightfully yours—*CHEAP FOOD AND*

DRINK! If you decide to dine upstairs, I have one suggestion: fondue. There is something about fondue that screams romance. Try it in cheese or chocolate . . . it will add a little spice to your evening.

ADDRESS 89 Winthrop Street, Harvard Square.

PHONE 491-1160.

HOURS Happy Hours: Sun–Thur 5–7 and 9:30–11; Fri 5–7 only.

PRICES All food $1.50; Beers $2.65–3.50!

DIRECTIONS From the Charles River, take JFK Boulevard two blocks to Winthrop Street. Grendel's is on the left behind the little park there.

By T: Take the Red Line to Harvard Square. At the exit by Out of Town Tickets, cross JFK Boulevard and walk toward the Charles River to the little park on the right. Grendel's is behind the park.

PARKING Happy Hours are the hardest hours to park in Harvard Square. You're better off T-ing it. But if you insist you can probably find a spot after 15–20 minutes of diligent scouting. Try some of the outer streets in the area.

MEXICAN CUISINE AT FOREST CAFE

So you want Mexican food, but you're tired of the typical variation of the same four ingredients wrapped in a different way? How about a restaurant that's heavy on the hot stuff and light on the wallet? Owned by the same people as The Porter House Cafe Texas Chili Parlor and Pit Bar-B-Que, the Forest Cafe has outrageously good food that's surprisingly creative. The restaurant is a neat little joint between Harvard Square and Porter Square with great atmosphere that's a combination of North Cambridge and Tijuana. Not too hard to imagine, huh? They've got a great selection of music that's loud enough to be interesting, but not so loud as to make it hard to talk.

Get ready for a lot of choices in the pesado y puerco department (translated fish and pork). Both are fantastic with endless choices of sauces and accompaniments. Personally I'd suggest choosing from their ample selection of daily specials of entrées and appetizers. They usually include details like fresh coriander sauce, hand-ground roasted tomatoes, mushroom, bacon, red wine, ancho and mulatto chili sauce. Entrées run $10–14 (specials are a little less)—a little steeper than your average Mexican grub, but when you lay your eyes and sink your teeth into these masterpieces, you'll know why. If you are interested in something a little cheaper and just as mouth-watering, try having an appetizer for the main dish. You can get something a little more basic like enchiladas, quesadillas or nachos, or you can branch out and try the oysters, calamares in chili or sopes, which is tortilla dough filled with chili sauce, fried beans, and Mexican cheese. The appetizers are only $2.50–6. If the hotness starts to get to you, cool off with one of their many drinks. Beers are $2–3. I suggest bottled beer because the draught glasses are pretty small. They also have an array of Oasis frozen drinks to choose from starting at $3.25—I always go for the regular margarita.

After dinner, if you're in the mood for ice cream, try Emack and Bolio's just down the street toward Porter Square. For a really cheap beer and interesting conversation pieces, there's Nick's Beef and Beer down the block near Emack's. And if you're in the mood for some live entertainment, Toad at 1920 Mass. Ave. in Porter Square has phenomenal live entertainment and a hip atmosphere every night of the week.

ADDRESS 2046 Mass. Ave., Cambridge.

PHONE 661-1634.

HOURS Open daily 5–10. Fri and Sat open until 10:30.

PRICES Appetizers: $2–6; Entrées: $10–14; Drinks: $3–5.

DIRECTIONS Go north on Mass. Ave. from Harvard Square and you'll find Mexican Cuisine at the Forest Cafe on the left side. Although the sign is a little hard to find, luckily it's a few doors before Nick's Beef and Beer's unmissable sign.

PARKING There's usually space available on the street at the meter spots. You may have to walk a bit.

By T: Take the Red Line to Harvard Square (or Porter Square) and walk about 15 minutes along Mass. Ave. toward Porter Square (or Harvard Square) and follow the above directions.

NICK'S BEEF AND BEER HOUSE

If it's smoky, loud and teeming with beef and beers, it's got to be Nick's Beef and Beer House. Although it's usually a little over-run by Harvard students, you can still find a colorful local over the age of 22. As for the ambiance: Nick's Beef and Beer House isn't exactly the "it's the first date and I really want to impress the girl" kinda place. It's more of a "hey, I know you, you know me, this place has gotta lotta color and a whole lotta bang for a buck." Let us say . . . rough and tumble.

When you go to Nick's, be really hungry for a stick-to-the-ribs dinner and a whole bunch of beer to wash it down with. Keep in mind that "beef" doesn't just mean burgers; they've got lamb chops, broiled steak, pork chops, fried shrimp, fried haddock, baked sausage, veal cutlet, hot pastrami, chicken wings and more. These delicacies go for $3–8, but most hover around $4.50. Then there are the burgers: the famous Double King Hamburger is only $3.15, and it's HUGE. If you're not that ambitious, try the regular (yet still King size) burger for $1.10. There's also an array of hot sandwiches that are all a huge undertaking: hot pastrami, imported salami, German frank, pepper steak and veal cutlet for $1.35–2.75. Hard to believe, but true.

To impress upon you exactly how much food you get for so little money, let me relay this true story. Recently, while at Nick's, I saw a man, an older, somewhat portly man eat an inordinate, and I mean INORDINATE, amount of food. We're talking burgers, salads, side dishes, maybe even a dessert, but I can't be certain. He also had plenty of drinks—enough so he was a mite wobbly on his way out. And when the bill came, I thought to myself, "This is going to he a hefty tab." The waitress walked over to the man and said (this is not a lie), "That'll be $6.25."

So, in conclusion I would like to state that Nick's Beef and Beer House is a fine choice if you are: a) familiar with your date, b) STARVING, c) ready to drink a lot of beer, and d) don't happen to have a lot of cash on hand.

ADDRESS 1688 Mass. Ave., Cambridge.

PHONE 492-4284.

HOURS Mon–Sun 11 a.m.–12 a.m.

PRICES Beef (and other entrées): $3–8; Beers: $1.50–3 ($4 pitchers).

DIRECTIONS Go north on Mass. Ave. from Harvard Square and Nick's is on the left side. Although the sign is enormous, it is old and currently reads: "Nick's _eef and Bee_ H__se." Don't be fooled, it's the real thing.

PARKING There's usually a space available on the street at the meter spots. There's an off-chance that you may have to walk a bit.

By T: Take the Red Line to Harvard Square (or Porter Square) and walk about 15 minutes down Mass. Ave. toward Porter Square (or Harvard Square), and follow the above directions.

REDBONES

". . . And now ladies and gentlemen, the winner in the category of Meat Chomping, Carnivore Craving, Blood Thirst Fulfillment is . . . REDBONES." It's not just an experience going to Redbones in Davis Square, its a whole new culture. Have you noticed that you haven't heard the word "macrobiotic" in a long time, but the phrase "big juicy steak" comes up quite a bit? Well, the rumors are true: meat is back. It is no longer fashionable to feign vegetarianism and deprive yourself of those pulled pork sandwiches while reaching for flimsy carrot sticks. If you are a vegetarian, there is a fantastic macrobiotic restaurant in the Porter Exchange Building in

Porter Square. And if you are a vegetarian, do *NOT* go to Red-bones. You won't enjoy yourself. There is this strange phenomenon that comes over people when they go to Redbones. It's like we revert back to our caveman ancestor days and just dig in with reckless abandon tearing into this meal in case it's our last. It's wild, and it's great to see people enjoy their food so completely. If you've been there you understand the enthusiasm for the grub—it's delicious. Southern delicacies are their specialty with fried okra, succotash, corn fritters and catfingers galore.

When it comes to the meat department, the treats just get better. You can get a Barbecue Beef Brisket Sandwich or Fried Catfish Sandwich (see, there isn't just meat!) for $6. If you want to order from the barbecue menu, the prices go up a bit ranging from $8 to $14, but the meals are fantastic. The sausage dinner is really special, and the wood-grilled chicken is another delight. But if you want to go with the traditional meat, I would suggest the Memphis Rack or Texas Beef Ribs or Baby Back Ribs. Or, if you can't decide, which I never can, you can get a combo of the three. This will run you about $13. I found that the Baby Backs were great, but a little puny to satisfy my meat needs, whereas the Arkansas Ribs were just the right amount to sink my teeth into.

Although you may want to stay for dessert at Redbones to choose between pecan and sweet potato pies, you could also try one of the myriad places in Davis Square. My new favorite for dessert is Rosebud's (see below). But you can also try Mikes Restaurant at 9 Davis Square or the Someday Cafe at 15 Davis Square next door to the Somerville Theater—which is, by the way, a great cheap place to see movies and shows.

ADDRESS 55 Chester Street, Davis Square, Somerville.

PHONE 628-2200.

PRICES Appetizers: $2–6; Entrées: $6–14; Drinks $1–4.

HOURS Open everyday 11 a.m.–12:30 a.m.

DIRECTIONS From Mass. Ave. take a right onto Day Street, go to the traffic light, take a right onto Elm Street and then the first right onto Chester Street, and Redbones is on the right. Chester Street follows through back to Mass. Ave., but it's one-way, so you need to take Day Street to get to it.

PARKING Davis Square is well endowed in the parking category, with plenty of municipal parking places that are free after 6. Otherwise, there are usually ample parking spots on the streets.

THE ROSEBUD DINER

You may have heard some strange rumors about the Rosebud Diner in the recent past, but let me assure you that Rosebud's is now up and running and in tiptop form. Maybe it's the little details that make Rosebud's so good, maybe it's the nice people and friendly service . . . but I gotta say, it's the great food at low prices that sends me back. In addition to being located in a 1940s railroad car, Rosebuds has a charming host named Teddy who greets you at the door with a weathered smile and elegantly leads you to your seat. Then there are the owners who are there until all hours of the night chatting with patrons and offering a complimentary drink or cigarette with the utmost sincerity.

To give you a little background and possibly explain why this restaurant seems to mean so much to the owners and all those who work there, the Rosebud Diner opened in 1941 and was purchased in 1958 by the current owners, the Nichols family. In 1986 it was sold to three men who defaulted on it in 1992. Since then, the Nichols family has repurchased it, renovated it and brought it up to date with a new back dining room and a second bar. No wonder going to the Rosebud Diner is more than just a yummy meal; it's like going home.

If you are expecting typical diner fare, you may be pleasantly surprised to find great innovations and variety, along with the old diner favorites. Because Rosebud's does such a good job with these newer items, like Grilled Artichokes ($6) and Grilled Italian Sandwich ($8), you really should branch out and try them. But if you are determined to stick with the old faithful, I would suggest one of the many delicious burgers—in particular, the Reuben Burger ($6) is out of this world. But be careful to save room for dessert because they have the best Boston Cream Pie I have ever eaten—and I don't usually even like Boston Cream Pie.

Other solid choices at Rosebud's are the House Specialties like the Mussels Fra Diavolo ($9) or the Beef or Lamb Shish-Kabob ($10). Surprisingly, Rosebud's also has a full bar—in fact it has two full bars, and some great beers on tap. I suggest the Red Ass beer for only $1.50 a pint. Can't beat that.

If you haven't ever been to the Rosebud Diner, give it a shot, and if you haven't been there in a while, it's time to give it another try.

ADDRESS 381 Summer Street, Davis Square, Somerville.

PHONE 666-6015.

HOURS Mon–Fri 9 a.m.–12:30 a.m.; Sat–Sun 8 a.m.–12:30 a.m.

PRICES Appetizers: $3–6; Entrées: $5–11; Drinks: $1–4.

DIRECTIONS From Mass. Ave. take a right onto Day Street, then take a right at the lights onto Elm Street. Follow Elm Street until you see the railroad car of the Rosebud Diner on your left.

PARKING As noted above, Davis Square has plenty of municipal parking, as well as meter spots that are free after 6.

HENRY'S DINER

When was the last time you had a meal in an authentic railroad car? Described as one of the "last surviving vestiges of true Americana," diner cars are always a blast; but combine that novelty with great diner food for low, low prices, and you've got yourself a real gem. Henry's tends to be slightly rough around the edges, but if diner food is beckoning, and you're not too concerned with impressing your date with optimal surroundings, Henry's is your spot.

The menu really tickles my fancy—in fact, my four favorite

words are found on Henry's menu: breakfast served all day. In case you're unfamiliar with the phrase, this means is that at any time of the day you can get their unbelievable raisin bread French toast, malted waffles, hashbrowns, eggs any way, pancakes, sausage, bacon, juice, muffins and hot and cold cereal for very little dough. Most breakfasts are about $3—and that serves up a lot of food.

But I shouldn't harp on breakfast when Henry's has so many other fine assets like diner subs and sandwich specials ($4–5). You can get one of Boston's finest reubens, a grilled tuna melt or the diner deli with ham, turkey and Swiss. Oceanside specials ($5–9) are also good, as well as the array of Greek specialties. Try the Greek pocket salad ($3) or gyros and kabobs ($4–5)—I don't know if Henry is Greek, but he certainly has mastered Greek cuisine!

Home plates are excellent: mac and cheese, franks and beans, Italian platter or knockwurst platter each for about $5. Daily specials are also a steal with anything from a meatloaf plate to steak usually priced at about $5. By the way, isn't it about time you gave meatloaf another try?

With such an old fashioned flair, its not surprising that Henry's only serves pies and ice cream for dessert—maybe an occasional pudding, but none of this fancy-schmancy mousse kind of stuff. In the same vein, Henry's offers fountain sodas, *bottled* Coca-Cola, frappes, milkshakes (remember, we're in New England where a frappe is made with ice cream and a milkshake is only milk and syrup), IBC rootbeer, ice cream floats and the good old bottomless cup of coffee. You gotta love diners!

Located on Western Avenue near North Harvard Avenue, Henry's is a great spot for a cheap bite to eat before you head into Harvard Square for some entertainment. If you're smart, you'll park nearby and then walk to Harvard Square—save yourself the parking headache.

ADDRESS 270 Western Avenue, Allston.

PHONE 783-5844.

HOURS Open weekdays 6 a.m.–9 p.m.; Saturdays 6 a.m.–7 p.m.; Sundays 6 a.m.–5 p.m.

PRICES Breakfast $2–5; Sandwiches: $2–5; Dinner Plates: $3–8; Desserts: $2–4.

DIRECTIONS From Boston, take the Storrow Drive exit at Western Avenue, take a left and follow Western Avenue to the major intersection with North Harvard Street. Go straight through intersection, passing Dunkin Donuts on the left, and continue to find Henry's about a quarter of a mile on the left side of Western Avenue.

By T/Bus: One of the best routes to Henry's is to take the Red Line to Harvard Square, then take the 86 Bus from Harvard Square to the first stop on Western Avenue. Another way is to take the 57 Bus from Kenmore Square to the corner of Brighton Avenue and Harvard Avenue. From there take the 66 Bus going toward Harvard Square to the stop at North Harvard Avenue and Western Avenue. Take a left onto Western Avenue to find Henry's about a quarter of a mile on the left side. Call the MBTA for other routes at 722-3200.

PARKING Henry's has a parking lot in back of the railroad car.

THE MIDDLE EAST RESTAURANT

Hailed for its great local music just about every night of the week, it's important to remember that the Middle East is also a fantastic restaurant with some of Boston's best Middle Eastern food at wonderfully cheap prices. The food goes beyond the typical humus and tabouli stuff. But to be fair, I have to say that theirs is the gosh darn best hummus (or hoomis, as they spell it) I have ever experienced—in fact, it so smooth and creamy that it's hard to believe it's the same stuff served elsewhere.

Sandwiches ($3–5) are a great bargain and let you experience some of their specialties without too much financial damage. The grilled vegetable sandwich is great, but the grape leaves sandwich is even better—both covered in tahini sauce and stuffed into a fresh

---

pita. Salads ($3.50) are impressive because they aren't the same old thing. Even the basic Greek salad is much better than I have had elsewhere. For a change of pace, try something like the fool m'dammas salad, which is a Middle Eastern specialty of cooked fava beans and chick peas.

Vegetarian entrées ($7–9) are very popular and interesting— you pretty much need a translator to figure what this stuff is. Pumpkin kibby labanich is a nutty little number with yogurt, mint and a whole bunch of garlic. Maklouta is an amazing stew with lots of beans and seasonings and good stuff. Msaah is an eggplant dish served with rice pilaf and bourgal (I've had this dish and I still don't know what the bourgal is!). If meat is what you're up for, you're still in luck because the Middle East serves up some of the meanest, meatiest dishes you can imagine. The novelty of shish kebabs ($9) will never wear off for me; it's like fondue, just so much fun to eat on a date and the Middle East does it very well.

Besides a very wide selection of foods, the Middle East also has a number of well-priced wines to choose from by the glass ($3–4) or the bottle ($11–14). Draught ($3–4) beers are also within our budget, and they serve some great ones like Saranac Black & Tan, Sam Adams and Harpoon. The Middle East also has pitchers of beer for around $10.

Another big hit at the Middle East is the weekend brunch served 10–4 on Saturdays and Sundays. You can choose from a large menu of Middle Eastern dishes like the Mafraket Batata ($6) and regular old American breakfasts like fresh fruit pancakes ($4).

Even if you've come to the Middle East for the food, you have to stay for the music. The restaurant has two eating sections (separated in the middle by an Indian restaurant) and a downstairs that used to be a bowling alley, where there is more live music. In the bakery the music is usually free and spotlights some of Boston's better local musicians. The other two areas for music tend to charge a cover. For more details on the Middle East's music scene, see entry in *Live Music* section.

ADDRESS 472 and 480 Mass. Avenue, Central Square, Cambridge

PHONE 354-8238. For music information: 492-0576.

HOURS Sun–Wed 11 a.m.–midnight. Thur–Sat 11 a.m.–1 a.m.

PRICES Appetizers: $2–4; Salads: $3–8; Entrées: $3–10; Drinks: $1–4; Desserts: $2–6.

DIRECTIONS From Boston take Mass. Ave. over the Mass. Ave. Bridge for about a mile to find the Middle East on the left side of the street.

By T: Take the Red Line to the Central Square station. Walk south on Mass. Ave. for two blocks to find the Middle East on the right side of the street.

PARKING There is usually some street parking available. Try the side streets.

LA FAMIGLIA

I believe that La Famiglia's reputation precedes itself, but in case you haven't yet heard how wonderful it is, get ready. There are so many impressive aspects to La Famiglia's three locations in the North End, Newbury Street, and East Boston, that it is hard to pinpoint exactly what makes it so fantastic. Putting aside the delicious food in giant portions, I have to say that the staff and the atmosphere that they create are really what make it a winner. The staff (or should I call them the family) will touch your shoulder when they speak to you, make suggestions, even bring over a dish of this or that to complement yours. Maybe now it's clear why they named it La Famiglia . . . throw in a bottle of wine and it's an Old World family reunion.

Prices are very reasonable. Appetizers are $3–7; I have to recommend the garlic bread. Entrées ($5–18) vary with pasta dishes of all kinds, seafood plates and other Italian delights. Beer is about $2–3, and wine is the average $13–25 per bottle.

But how is the food?

Honestly, the food is *OH-MY-GOODNESS* incredible. Every dish tastes as if your mother painstakingly slaved over it; the seasoning is perfect, and every bite seems to melt in your mouth. But I can't help admitting that I am very fond of the giant portions. My personal tactic is to not even try to finish the whole thing, but to take it home (you won't have to cook for days), and then save room for dessert. If you are at the North End or Newbury Street location, I strongly suggest that you skip dessert at La Famiglia and venture out to some of the local cafes for dessert, coffee and cordials. In the North End, try Cafe Vittoria at 296 Hanover Street or Mike's Pastry at 300 Hanover Street. On Newbury Street there are many different options including Ben and Jerry's at 174 Newbury Street or Emack and Bolio's at 290 Newbury Street.

A NOTE ON THE EAST BOSTON LOCATION: If you don't live near East Boston then you probably aren't so inclined to go out to this location. But here's a little incentive. The MBTA now offers a ferry that leaves from Long Wharf (at the Marriott Long Wharf Hotel) and goes directly to East Boston for only $1. It's wonderful. The ferries run year-round and in the off-season you get the ferry almost all to yourself. Stepping onto a ferry will make any drab date seem like you're in the heart of Venice. For more details see page 163.

ADDRESS 112 Salem Street, North End. 250 Newbury Street, Back Bay. 19 Bennington Street, South Boston.

PHONE 367-6711 (North End). 247-1569 (Back Bay). 569-4176 (East Boston).

HOURS 11–10:30 every day. Lunch menu is served 11–3; dinner is 4–10:30.

PRICES Entrées: $4–16; Appetizers: $3–7; Drinks $1–4. The wine list is the most expensive part at $13–25 per bottle.

DIRECTIONS North End: Salem Street, parallel to Hanover Street, is two or three blocks from Cross Street on the left side.

By T: The closest T station is Haymarket on the Orange Line. From the station, walk under the Central Artery and straight up Salem Street and follow above directions.

Newbury Street: La Famiglia is located on Newbury Street between Fairfield and Gloucester streets.

By T: Take the Green Line to the Hynes Convention Center stop. From the exit on Newbury Street, turn right and walk two and half blocks to find La Famiglia on the right side.

East Boston: From the Callahan Tunnel, take an immediate right out of the tunnel and follow to the set of lights (Santarpio's Pizza is in front of you), take a left, go under the overpass to lights and take another left. Pass the toll booths on your left and keep going straight past Lombardo's on the left to the second stop sign at Bennington Street, and take a right to find La Famiglia on your right side.

PARKING North End: La Famiglia's validated parking deal at All Right Parking under the Central Artery is a must. Bring the ticket and get it validated at the restaurant. Parking is about $1 an hour. Nice!

Newbury Street: Parking is really difficult, so you are better off taking the T—even driving to a T station that has parking and taking the T from there. If you insist on driving, go early enough to drive around the side streets for an open spot.

East Boston: Parking is available on the street and also in the lot across the street.

LA PICCOLA VENEZIA

I was reluctant to try the new Piccola Venezia on Hanover Street because I liked the old one on Salem Street so much. But what I discovered is that for a dollar or two more, the new Piccola Venezia has even better food in an upscale and gorgeous atmosphere. There is still the same homey charm of the old place, but now you're dining in style . . . this place is *swank*. While the food used to be large portioned but somewhat unrefined, now the menu has much more ingenuity, it's flavorful, and as always, it's made to order. The pasta dinners are now divine ($6–15), and the seafood ($10–18) is better than ever. Daily specials have the most spunk. If you're smart you won't fill up on the warm bread, but I can't resist one of their yummy appetizers ($2–8). Still you must save room for the Italian-style huge entrées. One of the best parts of Piccola Venezia is ordering polenta instead of pasta with your dinner; it's a real treat. Don't forget to take your leftovers home!

I love restaurants where you can order a pitcher of wine ($9–12); it's the most economical way to drink. If you are set on having dessert at La Piccola Venezia you will be impressed, but might I suggest a stroll around the neighborhood and a pastry and cappuccino?

ADDRESS 263 Hanover Street, North End.

PHONE 523-3888.

HOURS 11:30–10 daily (kitchen stays open a little later on Friday and Saturday nights).

DIRECTIONS On Hanover Street near the Central Artery, La Piccola Venezia is one of the first restaurants on the right side of this North End thoroughfare.

By T: Haymarket station on the Orange Line is the closest stop. From the station walk under the Central Artery, take a right onto Cross Street, pass Martignetti's and then a left onto Hanover Street.

PARKING Thank goodness for validated parking! Park at the All Right Parking Lot, under the Central Artery near the entrance to the Callahan Tunnel. Bring your ticket to get validated for about $1 per hour.

BUDDHA'S DELIGHT

Delight indeed! Buddha's Delight is one of the few restaurants in Chinatown that serves all vegetarian food. But what's even more interesting is that when you read the menu, you will find dishes such as pork lo-mein and beef fried with lemon grass. Confused? Buddha's serves what's called mock-meats, using substitutes like gluten and tofu served with heaps of exquisite vegetables, rice and noodles. You can even get an entire mock lobster (had the B-52s only been to Buddha's!) entirely made of gluten and entirely edible—even the shell! I was a skeptic when I first entered Buddha's, but honestly, I can't tell the difference from real meats. Despite being all vegetarian, the menu remains quite the same as other restaurants in the area. There is a full pork, seafood and chicken assortment—all the dishes are spectacular and incredibly cheap. Their vermicelli dishes are out of this world ($4–7) and noodle soups ($3–5) deserve commendation, as well as the poultry tofu (all about $7).

Another specialty of Buddha's Delight are the assortment of cold beverages. You can get all sorts of exotic milk shakes, coconut, plum, lemon and coffee drinks for around $2. They shouldn't be passed up.

Buddha's Delight is also available for take-out!

ADDRESS 5 Beach Street, Chinatown.

PHONE 451-2395.

PRICES Appetizers: $3–5; Entrées: $4–8; Drinks: $1–2.

HOURS Open daily 11–10. Open until 11 on Friday and Saturday.

DIRECTIONS Even if you are unfamiliar with Chinatown, Buddha's is easy to find at the corner of Washington Street and Beach Street across from the former Naked Eye side entrance.

By T: The closest stop is on the Orange Line at the Chinatown station. Head towards Washington Street, take a left and then another left onto Beach Street. The Boylston Street station on the Green Line is not too far either. From the station, walk up Boylston Street, take a right onto Washington Street, and then a left onto Beach Street. This is not always the safest area to be walking around at night.

PARKING For the most part, Chinatown has decent parking options. If one is not available on Beach Street, try one of the side streets. Be advised to not leave valuables in your car.

SIAM SQUARE

Although Siam Square is just one of the many cheap restaurants in Chinatown, I prefer it over many others because of its cleanliness, good service and wonderful menu of Thai foods. Start off with one of their fabulous appetizers ($3–5) like the shredded nutty taro root shaped into nests with light crispy batter, fried and served with sweet chili sauce. Thai rolls are good too, but I'd try the Thai sticks of fried zucchini, yams and green beans served with a great peanut sauce. Soups ($2–3) also make great appetizers, especially the chicken coconut soup or shrimp hot and sour soup spiced with lemon grass, chili, lime juice and straw mushrooms. Hot hot!

Moving on to the entrées, I would definitely order two dishes and split them—everything is too good to experience just one dish! The noodle menu ($5–6) is great, but I can hardly ever force myself to order anything but the divine Pad Thai. The healthy vegetarian Ba-Mee is great too with assorted vegetables, fried noodles and soy sauce. Chef's Specialties ($6–8) deliver a lot of fresh vegetables served over a steaming mound of rice. The chicken cashew nuts with chunks of pineapple and scallions or the beef macadamia with nuts in a ginger sauce are particular favorites. If you're a pork fan, you've got to experience the wild boar basil sautéed in spicy chili sauce.

Curry dishes are fantastic, but it's hard to choose from the green, yellow, red or masaman curry—then you have to choose chicken, beef, shrimp or duck. Since there are a lot of choices to make, might I suggest trying the duck? And, as if that weren't enough to choose from, you can also combine your own selection of any meat with any vegetable (baby corns, ginger, hot basil leaves, pineapple, spicy bamboo shoots—just to name a few) to create your own heaven.

Siam Square serves a variety of cold beverages along with hot teas. Both Thai beer and Heineken are available for $ 3.75.

ADDRESS 86 Harrison Avenue, Chinatown.

PHONE 338-7704.

HOURS Open daily 11:30–11.

PRICES Appetizers: $3.50–5; Entrées: $5–8; Drinks: $1–4.

DIRECTIONS Located at the corner of Kneeland Street and Harrison Avenue in the heart of Chinatown.

By T: The closest stop is on the Orange Line at the Chinatown station. From the exit walk towards Harrison Avenue, take a right, and walk about three blocks to find Siam Square on the left side. The Boylston Street station on the Green Line is not too far either. From the station, walk up Boylston Street, take a right onto Harrison Avenue, and follow the above directions. This is not always the safest area to be walking around at night. Perhaps a cab to and from the T is best.

PARKING Parking is difficult in Chinatown, but not altogether impossible. Be patient and try the side streets. Be prepared to walk a few blocks.

BREW MOON

If you've dressed for a night at the theater and have already shelled out the cash for theater tickets, the last thing you want to do is drop a chunk of change at a restaurant. But then again, slumming in fancy clothes ain't too romantic either. Brew Moon offers a pretty perfect alternative. The atmosphere is upscale, the fare puts a refreshing spin on old favorites and the prices are quite reasonable—especially if you stay away from some of the higher priced entrées. Appetizers are hefty and range about $3–7. For an interesting alternative to nachos and buffalo wings, try the classic buffalo roaster wings and smoked chicken nachos. The appetizer list also features some original and very creative dishes like apple wood salmon, hearty lamb tenderloin and grilled portabello mushroom.

Salads are excellent ($4–9), but are quite large, so you may want to split one or make it your whole meal. Try the Roquefort salad with grilled shrimp or the haymarket salad with grilled chicken, onions, romano, potato crouton, and warm roasted garlic. In the way of sandwiches, you can choose from burgers to pastrami ($6–8), but don't expect the same old same old. Their smothered burger is quite literally smothered in Boursin or blue cheese. And, as for the pastrami, how about toasted sourdough, melted Swiss and pommery mustard cream? If you're hungry and willing to spend a few more bucks, choose an entrée like brew house battered flounder ($9), spiced bronzed swordfish ($16) or molasses and cumin-charred pork tenderloin ($15)—do and you'll leave a little poorer, but very fulfilled.

Besides being a fine restaurant, Brew Moon is also a microbrewery and has a terrific selection of handcrafted beers. If you aren't familiar with any of them, start off with the lunar sampler: 4-oz. shots of five of their best beers for $5.50. It's a better buy than beer by the pint, and it makes for great conversation—you can have your own private beer tasting. Other beers are all about $3.50, and range greatly in darkness and flavor. Wines are also available by the glass ($4–6) and the bottle ($14–30). If you are in the mood for dessert, I have to emphasize how good the brewer's root beer float is. Incidentally, Brew Moon is also a good spot to stop just for dessert and coffee after a show or anytime you're in the neighborhood.

One of the greatest things about Brew Moon is the live music for no cover. Stop in even if you aren't staying for dinner. Order a lunar sampler and have your beer tasting with live guitar music. Call ahead to see find out who's on and when.

Note: New Brew Moon locations are opening since the original met with such success. As of press date there were new Brew Moon locations in Cambridge on Church Street and in Saugus on

Route 1. If they follow in the footsteps of the original, they will be great successes.

ADDRESS 115 Stuart Street, Theater District.

PHONE 523-6467.

PRICES Appetizers: $5–7; Entrées: $6–18; Drinks: $2–5.

HOURS Daily 11:30 a.m.–11 (open until 2 a.m. on weekends). Kitchen closes at 11.

DIRECTIONS Brew Moon is on the corner of Stuart and Tremont streets in the heart of the Theater District.

By T: From the Boylston Street station, walk down Tremont Street away from Boston Common to Stuart Street.

PARKING Don't even try to park unless you want to turn your Cheap Date into an expensive one. If you do drive, plan on parking in Chinatown and walking, or paying excessively at the garages.

FAJITAS & 'RITAS

Fajitas & 'Ritas may not be for everyone, but if you love fajitas and you love margaritas, you've come to the right spot. They have two locations, both of which offer particular benefits: in Brookline you get parking; in Downtown Crossing you get some interesting people and a swinging after-work crowd. The theme of both seems to be along the lines of kindergarten. Let me explain: besides having paper tablecloths and buckets of crayons so you can practice your drawing (don't forget to stay in the lines), the entire menu is an exercise with building blocks. You get an order form filled with options, then you build your own fajitas ($6–12): start with the basics (shrimp, steak, chicken or vegetable) and then add what you like (extra cheese, guacamole, pico de gallo sauce, beans, you name it). Nachos ($5–8) are the same: check off exactly what you want to build your own dream nachos. The genius of this setup is that you get exactly what you want in your food, and pay for only that.

Daily specials are also innovative—have you ever experienced a turkey fajitas?

The margaritas follow this same vain: check off exactly how you want it (regular, strawberry, with salt, on the rocks, frozen, etc.). Margaritas are always expensive, but at Fajitas & 'Ritas you can get margaritas starting at $3—and they're delicious. They also feature a daily margarita special—no turkey margaritas, but how about raspberry, banana, or cranberry?

If you want to hang out afterwards, the West Street location has a fun bar area with an extensive list of beers.

ADDRESS 25 West Street, Downtown Boston; 48 Boylston Street, Brookline Village.

PHONE 426-1222 (Downtown).
566-1222 (Brookline).

HOURS Downtown: Open weekdays 11:30–9; Thur open until 10; Fri open until 11. Sat noon–10. Closed Sundays.

Brookline: Mon 5–9; Tue–Thur 5–10; Fri 11:30–11; Sat noon–11; Sun 5–10.

PRICES Nachos: $5–8; Fajitas: $6–12; 'Ritas: $3–6.

DIRECTIONS Downtown: West Street runs perpendicular to Tremont and Washington streets near Downtown Crossing. From Tremont Street, walk down West Street and Fajitas & 'Ritas is on the left side about halfway between the two streets.

By T: The closest T station is Park Street although Boylston Street is a close second. From the Park Street exit walk down Tremont Street past Temple Street and take a left onto West Street. The restaurant is about halfway down the street on the left.

Brookline: Located right on Route 9 in Brookline, Fajitas & 'Ritas is next door to Carvel Ice Cream.

By T: Take the Green Line's D train to Brookline Village. Walk down Harvard Street to Route 9 (Boylston Street), cross the street and find the restaurant near Carvel Ice Cream, across from Brookline Savings Bank.

PARKING Downtown: Parking is very difficult. If you insist on driving be prepared to walk from your parking spot. Try along Tremont Street.

Brookline: There is plenty of parking on the street.

SMALL PLANET

"We live on a small planet where far more unites us than divides us. May we all sow, may we all reap and may we all share and enjoy the harvest." I know of many restaurants that tout virtuous intentions such as these, but stop there. At Small Planet, not only do they have aim to educate, but they also contribute 10 percent of their profits to hunger-related charities. Compound that with great fresh food, a fantastic interior, and decent prices—you've got yourself all the makings of a great hangout. You can choose from a list of Square Meals ($9–13) and Feasts ($14–16), or stick to the Small Menu ($3–9) where prices are more in our range. If you're really splurging and decide to order from the Square Meals or Feasts menus, you can choose things like grilled vegetable lasagna ($10), Asian stir fry noodles ($9) or paella de casa ($16) with shrimp, clams, mussels, chicken, charico sausage and saffron rice, all of which are delectable and big enough to be shared between two people. Personally, these prices are out of my budget, so I usually choose both appetizers and entrées from the Small Menu. I've spent many hours at Small Planet and have had just about everything on the menu, so it's hard for me to rave about only a few of the items. Thai shrimp noodles ($8) with peanut sauce is fabulous; quesadilla ($6) with vegetable, black beans or chicken is tangy and affordable; roasted root vegetable and chevre salad ($7) is from heaven and the Asian steamed mussels ($6) packs a powerful flavor. The bruschetta is a mountain of fresh bread topped with tomatoes, fresh basil and garlic, dribbled with olive oil—the perfect accompaniment to any entrée. If burgers are your thing, you're in for a surprise. Not content to offer the simple beef burger and maybe a slice of cheese, Small Plant has got turkey, vegetable and even a giant portabello mushroom burger with pesto. With these you can have either sharp Vermont cheddar or blue cheese, along with a plate full of hand-cut fries. Pizzas ($7–9) are a big deal at Small Planet and large enough to serve two. Aztec, sausage, white and Greek pizzas are also there for the choosing, and are teaming with sassy toppings like jalapeno, avocado, black olive tapenade and goat cheese.

As if the food weren't enough to get you running to Small Planet, the interior is (no pun intended) out of this world! Statues, waterfalls, clouded ceilings and wild animals fill this place with the most unexpected conversation pieces. There is a long bar where it's a pleasure to wait for your date and chat with the friendly bartender. The Small Planet bar area gets pretty jammed with an after-work crowd, but even so, it's rarely a wait for a table. There is a wide selection of beers on tap and in bottles ($3–4), along with a fine selection of wines by the glass ($3–5) and by the bottle ($14–25).

If you like the sound of Small Planet, but wish there was something like it in Cambridge, you're in luck. Rumor has it that Small Planet is opening another location in Cambridge. Hurray!

Here's a tip: Nothing starts a date off better than a small bouquet of fresh cut flowers from Winston's. Located next door, Winston's will guarantee you make a good impression.

ADDRESS 565 Boylston Street, Copley Square.

PHONE 536-4477.

HOURS Open daily 11:30 a.m.–1 a.m., except Mondays 5 p.m.–1 a.m.

PRICES Appetizers: $3–9; Entrées: $5–16; Drinks: $1–5.

DIRECTIONS In the heart of Copley Square, Small Planet is nestled between Winston Flowers and Clarendon Wine Co.

By T: Take the Green Line to Copley station. From the exit walk up Boylston Street toward Trinity Church to find Small Planet on the left side of the street. The Orange Line's Back Bay station is nearby as well.

PARKING If you are crazy enough to try to drive, arrive early enough to drive around for about half an hour to find a meter parking spot.

BAJA CANTINA

An upbeat, friendly atmosphere and a menu that offers more innovation and selection than most other Mexican restaurants makes this one stand out above the rest. The interior is brightly decorated with funky details, interesting designs and cozy booths and tables. As for food, you'll have to decide from a whole array of delicacies. Appetizers are yummy but hardly necessary, since portions are large, service is fast and chips and salsa are provided free upon request. Salads and cold tortillas range from $3 to $8 and are fabulous. Instead of a heavy appetizer, try splitting a char-grilled skirt steak salad with roasted peppers and pinto beans, or an avocado tortilla with honey-lime dressing—making sure to save room for what's next.

Entrées are under $13, and pack a powerful mouthful of flavor. Grilled tortillas are escorted by whole roasted anaheim peppers with spicy sweet potato sticks. Chimichangas ($8) are delicious with mouthfuls of chicken and Colby cheese. Both the three-grain burrito ($7) and the grilled vegetable burrito ($7) are good examples of Baja's innovation. To ensure that you truly have the Mexican experience, have either a margarita or sangria made exactly as you like it.

ADDRESS 111 Dartmouth Street, South End/Copley Square.

PHONE 262-7575 or 800-728-7570.

HOURS Sun–Thur 11:30–11; Fri and Sat 11:30 a.m.–12:30 a.m. (kitchen closes at 11:30).

PRICES Appetizers: $2–8; Entrées: $7–13; Drinks: $1–5.

DIRECTIONS From Boylston Street driving toward downtown take a right at Exeter Street, then a left onto Huntington Avenue. At the next lights on Dartmouth Street take a right and follow to find Baja on the left side past the Back Bay train station.

By T: Back Bay station on the Orange Line is just half a block (toward Columbus Avenue) from Baja. Copley station on the Green Line is just a bit farther. From Copley station on Boylston Street take a right onto Dartmouth Street and follow past the Back Bay station to find Baja a bit farther on the left side.

PARKING Virtually impossible! If you have anything to purchase at Copley Place, you can park in there for free after 5 p.m and get your ticket validated with a $5 purchase. Otherwise, you'll finding yourself searching Columbus Avenue and surrounding streets for a long time before you get a spot.

MOKA

Moka, on the border of Copley Square and the South End, has become a real favorite for the cash-conscious population in Boston. Moka calls itself a California Cafe because of its combination of vegetarian-style dishes (although they are not afraid to add meat to dishes) and its fresh, funky decor. The food is delicious and amply portioned. The atmosphere is extremely casual, with booths, intimate tables and stools on a windowed bar. There is self-service for those of us who prefer to act as our own waiters, as well as sit-down service.

The menu consists of a chic combination of sandwiches, pizzettes, salads, soups and many daily specials. The menu changes somewhat frequently, but you can usually expect to find things like homemade hummus and pita ($4), baked brie with fresh fruits ($5), vegetarian black bean chili ($4) and some meal-sized fresh salads ($3–7).

Moka's sandwiches add a new twist on old favorites, with things like a chicken sandwich adorned with spinach pesto, fresh tomatoes and provolone ($5), or tuna with roasted red pepper dressing, alfalfa sprouts, red onions and cucumbers ($4). Scrumptious! Pizzettes, too, show a particular ingenuity of taste. My favorite is the pizzette with spinach pesto, feta, tomatoes and mozzarella ($5)— a symphony of delectable flavors. Another delight is the roasted garlic, tomato, fresh basil and mozzarella pizzette; a bit more subtle than the other.

Moka's menu also offers a few hot dishes ($5–9) like a quesadilla with black beans, chicken, corn and cheese (for the most part, though, they leave the Mexican cuisine to their cousin across the way at Baja), or baked tortellini with pesto cream sauce and fresh tomatoes and even layered eggplant with herb cheese, tomato and provolone. Since the portions are large and it's likely that there are many menu items you'll want to try, it may be smart to order two dishes that you both like, and split them.

If you want something cold to wash it all down, order one of their inexpensive cold brews for $2.75–3.50 or a glass of wine. Personally, I find that one of their unique coffees ($1–4) hits the spot best; try the coffee bomb or almond milk. Add a dessert or two and you have the perfect ending to a meal.

Copley Square abounds with activities that would complement your date nicely; there are free concerts to hear, libraries and churches to peruse, and even a Winston Flowers to buy your sweetheart some sweet peas. Check the papers ahead of time to see what's going on and what's *FREE*!

ADDRESS 130 Dartmouth Street, Copley Square/South End.

PHONE 424-7768.

HOURS Mon–Fri 7–11; Sat and Sun 8–11.

PRICES Entrées: $5–7; Appetizers: $3–5; drinks: $1–3.50.

DIRECTIONS Moka is convenient to Copley Place (by Neiman Marcus), directly across from the Back Bay train station.

By T: The closest T stop is across the street on the Orange Line at Back Bay. Moka is also close to Copley station on the Green Line. From the Copley exit walk up Dartmouth Street toward Copley Place, pass it and keep walking until you reach Moka on the right, before Tent City apartment complex.

PARKING Parking is rather difficult in this area. After 5 p.m. you can park in the Copley Place Garage for free if you purchase something at the mall for more than $5 (movie tickets included). This may be a good time to buy your date some sweets at one of the mall's candy stores. Make sure to take your parking ticket with you for validation. Otherwise try to find a meter spot in the neighborhood.

CACTUS CLUB

I admit, the Cactus Club is neither the cheapest restaurant in Boston nor the most original choice for this chapter, but there is something about the Cactus Club's combination of hip location and atmosphere, tasty unique foods and array of drinks that makes it a perfect date restaurant. The Cactus Club acquired a new chef and revamped their menu in the past couple of years, which has made all the difference in their food. The new menu features delicacies like Cajun Catfish ($11), a Spanish Paella ($12) and many vegetarian meals like Burritos with Mosa ($10) and Mile High Mesa with Southwest Caesar Salad ($10). Yes, these are some of their most expensive entrées, but they're beautiful and extraordinarily tasty! Definitely worth the occasional splurge. But lets not go overboard: the Cactus' cheaper fare is great, too. They still have their famous Cactus Burger (8 oz. for $6) and an assortment of nachos. Plus their drinks are tons o' fun. The two of you can share a huge Cactus Bowl, a large concoction of Tequila, rum and something else I can't remember . . . anyway, it's great and makes the date interesting.

Outdoor seating is a big plus on a nice night when you can watch the Boylston Street clientele saunter, cruise, parade, etc. If you're not starved, then one of their huge appetizers will be enough for the two of you to split. The Cactus Club runs midday specials every so often, like half off their entire entrée menu weekdays, 4:30–6:30. Call ahead and ask what they've got to offer.

The fascinating decor is great if your date is low on dialogue. The bar is lively and tends to fill up with the Thursday, Friday and Saturday night crowds. But the restaurant section is very spacious and there is rarely a wait. The Cactus Club won Best of Boston's Meeting Spot Award in 1991. The award is no longer given; as one employee says, "They retired our number."

ADDRESS 939 Boylston Street, Boston.

PHONE 236-0200.

HOURS Open daily 11:30–2. The kitchen is open until 11.

PRICES Appetizers: $5–8; Entrées: $5–15; Drinks $3–7.

DIRECTIONS On Boylston Street across from the Hynes Convention Center at the Prudential.

By T: Take the Green Line to Hynes Convention Center/Auditorium. From the Mass. Ave. exit turn left and take another left onto Boylston Street. The Cactus Club is on the corner of Boylston and Hereford streets.

PARKING Parking is most difficult during the day and Thursday–Saturday nights. Your best bet is to drive around until you find meter parking. Be patient: one will turn up. Often, there are spots available on Boylston Street between Mass. Ave. and Hereford Street just before the ICA. If all else fails, there is pay parking down Boylston Street at the Prudential Center.

SORENTO'S

Sorento's is the perfect place to take a date when you want dinner to be the main event of the evening. You wouldn't want to rush in and out, wolfing down this incredible food. As is probably obvious from the name, Sorento's specializes in Italian cuisine, gourmet style. Since the food is so lovely, I would suggest ordering two entrées and splitting them; it's all too good to experience just one dish.

The pizzas are wonderful, with creative toppings like fried eggplant, prosciutto and fontinella cheese—and you can create your own. But I have to admit, the pizzas are not their best dish; the pasta is out of this world! All the ingredients are fresh and no dish is ever lacking in taste or uniqueness. Most pastas are about $10. Try Rigatoni Milano with prosciutto, mushrooms, onions and red bell peppers sautéed in olive oil and vodka. BRAVA! If you want something a little more basic, those dishes are less expensive.

Their calzones are also delightful. If you want to try it, but not for your meal, split one for an appetizer. You won't be disappointed. But when it comes to appetizers, the antipasto tops the list, packed with fresh meats, vegetables and cheeses.

The restaurant has many of the same qualities as Bluestone Bistro, with a slightly more elegant appeal. During the warmer months, you can sit outside and enjoy the evening. The interior is quite tiny, but rather romantic with dim lighting. Weeknights are great because there is rarely a wait, and because it's less crowded so you can sit and linger over your meal. Make sure to get the leftovers for home! Sorento's is also available for take-out and has *FREE* delivery.

ADDRESS 86 Peterborough Street, Fenway.

PHONE 424-7070.

HOURS Mon–Fri 11–12 a.m. Sat 1–12. Sun 2–12.

PRICES Appetizers: $3–9; Pizzas: $8–16; Pasta Dishes: $7–15.

DIRECTIONS The one-way Peterborough Street is located directly behind the Star Market on Boylston Street in the Fenway area. Coming from the intersection with Brookline Avenue and Park Drive, pass Star Market and take the next possible right, then another right onto Peterborough Street. Sorento's is up the block on the left.

PARKING Since parking can be tough on the street, Sorento's has a deal with the Boston Cab Company to let customers park on their lot for $3. After passing Sorento's (and looking adeptly for a free spot), take a left and go down the block towards Queensberry Street to find the Boston Cab Company on the left.

ANCHOVIES

Over the past few years, Anchovies in the South End has earned its reputation as a fun and funky little hole in the wall that, despite its small capacity, packs a real wallop with its tasty, wholesome and very cheap Italian food. The only downside is that because of its well deserved popularity, there tends to be a decent wait for tables on weekends. The good thing is that waiting is a pleasure thanks to the abundance of interesting people and great prices on beers and drinks! (Try a martini with "tom-olives.") The menu is somewhat basic, but filled with choices. Appetizers are worth a couple of bucks; try the antipasto for two or more people ($8), or the Italian nachos ($6). If you're not going to have an appetizer, you've got to at least allow yourself the garlic bread ($2).

As for the main dishes, there are a few different pastas: red sauce, meat sauce, garlic and oil, white clam and Italian sweet sausage; all for $5 to $8. Anchovies also has sandwiches filled with meats, sausage, and chicken cutlets ($5), but if you really want to get their specialty, order the pizza. Pizzas and calzones are about $5 for the basic and then an array of toppings for a bit more. The house specialty is, yes, you guessed it, anchovies. If anchovies aren't in your future, try some of the other toppings like artichoke hearts, roasted peppers, olives and sausage. Delicious!

Drinks at Anchovies are reasonable—which makes it a good watering hole even if you're not hungry. Beers run $2–4 and a glass of wine starts at $2.50. A fine, though small, selection of wines are offered by the bottle for $12–20. After dinner, you can always wander over to Mass. Ave. and see what's shaking at Wally's. One of the biggest assets about Anchovies is that it is one of the few restaurants in Boston that has a kitchen open late. It doesn't close until 1 a.m., and the bar stays open until 2 a.m.

ADDRESS 433 Columbus Avenue, South End.

PHONE 266-5088.

HOURS Open daily 4–2 a.m. Kitchen is open until 1 a.m. Last call is around 1:40 a.m.

PRICES Appetizers: $2–8; Pasta, sandwiches, pizzas and calzones: $5–10. Drinks: $2–4.

DIRECTIONS From Mass. Ave., take a left onto Columbus Avenue to find Anchovies a few blocks up on the left near Charlie's Sandwich Shoppe.

By T: Take the Orange Line to the Mass. Ave. station, walk down Mass. Ave. and follow the above directions. Symphony station and the Hynes Convention Center, both on the Green Line, are just a few blocks farther down Mass. Ave. than the Orange Line station. Walking from any of these stations at night is not always safe. Cabs are ample in the area.

PARKING The South End is equipped with visitor parking spots and a generous amount of non-residential spots on certain side streets; but it's still less than desirable to drive.

CHARLIE'S SANDWICH SHOPPE

The people at Charlie's Sandwich Shoppe in the South End may very well be the originators of homestyle cookin'. The menu is a combination of your basic greasy spoon options with a few unexpected surprises. Open since 1927, Charlie's has done so well for itself that it doesn't even have to stay open for dinner. You can get breakfast and lunch—and lots of it. Charlie's is the perfect spot for a Saturday brunch, a before-work breakfast date, or to complement those special days when you take off from work to explore Boston's day entertainment offerings.

Breakfasts consist of huge mouth-watering omelets ($5–7);

choose from Cajun, Western and the like, with hordes of hashbrowns on the side. Or a platter full of French toast slathered in blueberry compote ($4). Hot griddle cakes are a good old standby or be a little experimental and try the banana French toast.

If lunch is what you're in for, then choose from a variety of sandwiches, burgers, salads, chili and fish platters. The burgers are authentic patties piled high with tomatoes and lettuce, on a bulkie roll with a ton of fries for about $4. Sandwiches that sound basic and boring on the menu are mighty impressive to the hungry eyes and mouth. The variety of sandwiches is wide, ranging from liverwurst ($3) to ham and egg ($3.25) to hot roast beef ($5). Beverages are cheaper than most places, with cans of soda for $.70. The diner decor of Charlie's consists of personal photographs covering the walls, including a few celebrity patrons here and there. Requests like "no smoking" and "no unnecessary noise" make Charlie's the kind of place where it's nice to hang out. Plus there is no denying that the service is, well, kind of like family.

ADDRESS 429 Columbus Avenue, South End.

PHONE 536-7669.

HOURS Mon–Fri 6 a.m.–2.30 p.m.; Sat 7:30 a.m.–1 a.m.; *CLOSED SUNDAYS*, unfortunately.

PRICES Breakfast dishes: $3–6. Omelets: $5–7. Sandwiches: $3–5.

DIRECTIONS Charlie's is in the South End on Columbus Avenue between Braddock Parkway and Holyoke Street.

By T: The closest T stop is the Mass. Ave. station on the Orange Line. From the exit take a left onto Mass. Ave. and then another left onto Columbus Avenue, walk about five blocks and you'll find Charlie's on the left side.

PARKING Although it can be difficult to park in this neighborhood, there are a few visitor parking spots on the side streets. If you go for an early morning breakfast, you should have no trouble.

VILLAGE SMOKEHOUSE

If you like barbecued Texas-style grub, and you want a lot of it at a modest price, head on over to the Village Smokehouse in Brookline Village. It gets pretty crowded on weekends because people have heard that it's the best in town—some even say that it's better than Redbones in Davis Square, but I like them both for different reasons. While you wait for your table, you can watch them barbecue the food, slathering on their famous barbecue sauce while flames jump dangerously high.

Despite being only Texan, the menu is chock full of choices: pork or beef ribs ($11), a half chicken ($9), Texas sausage ($7), shrimp ($11), fajitas ($12) and all kinds of steaks ($10–14). For a less pricey entrée, have a burger ($5–7) bathed in their tasty barbecue sauce and served with pinto beans and a side dish of your choice. Make sure to ask for cornbread: it's free, and the perfect accompaniment to anything on the menu. However, make sure not to fill up on the appetizers and cornbread as the portions are giant. You and your date may want to split an order of the savory (and messy) ribs, thereby saving room for a slice of the heavenly apple pie.

The Village Smokehouse also offers some mean take-out. Grab some chow and go on a picnic to the Emerald Necklace or Jamaica Pond.

ADDRESS 1 Harvard Street, Brookline Village.

PHONE 566-3782 or call LONE STAR.

HOURS Mon–Thur 11:30–10; Fri and Sat 11:30–11; Sun 4–10.

PRICES Appetizers: $3–6; Entrées: $7–15; Burgers: $6.50; Beers and drinks: $1–4; Desserts: $3.

DIRECTIONS From Boston on Route 9 (Huntington Avenue turns into Route 9 at South Huntington Avenue), take a right before Brookline Savings Bank onto Harvard Street. The Smokehouse is three blocks on the right side.

By T: The T is a great way to get to Brookline Village. Take the Green Line D train to Brookline Village. From the station walk up to Harvard Street, take a right and find the Smokehouse two blocks up on the right side.

PARKING Parking can be tough—but still not as bad as downtown! There is meter parking on the streets, or meter lots (*FREE* after 6) behind Harvard Street.

MI VAMI

Tucked away into the recesses of Coolidge Corner, Mi Vami is a little neighborhood secret that serves exceptional food at really low prices. In fact, prices have barely been raised over the past ten years. Until recently the stark interior was the only drawback to Mi Vami, but now they have effectively redecorated this one-room restaurant to create a romantic oasis.

Make sure you're hungry when you step out to Mi Vami; not only do you get salad or fries and rice with all their dinners (about $8 each), but they give you an enormous main dish. If you are not in the mood for one of those large beef, chicken or lamb dinners, then try one of their cheaper, although not much smaller, sandwiches. I suggest the Falafel sandwich ($4). It's amazing what Mi Vami can fit into a pita! If you want to try a few different items, but know you don't have the room, split one of their well-sized appetizers ($4–5) and a dinner with your date. Approximate damage with sodas, coffee and desserts: $20. Hard to beat!

Mi Vami doesn't serve alcohol, but it is a "Bring Your Own Booze" joint, so don't forget to bring a bottle of your favorite wine or beer. If you forget to BYOB, there is a decent liquor store around the corner on Beacon Street. Other drinks are between $.90 and $1.50. When you come, you must stay for dessert ($1.50–4): baklava is out of this world and the cheesecake is a close second. Mi Vami also supplies take-out just in case you want to utilize your own homey ambiance.

Coolidge Corner is always a treat to stroll around after dinner.

There are a couple of book stores and excellent frozen yogurt at JP Licks on Harvard Avenue. Don't forget the Coolidge Corner Cinema is there too, with its fantastic selection of old and new movies.

ADDRESS 14A Pleasant Street, Brookline.

PHONE 277-0272.

HOURS Sun–Fri 4–10; Sat noon–11.

PRICES Appetizers: $3.50–4.50; Dinners: $7–10; Sandwiches: $3.50–4.50; Drinks: $1–1.50.

DIRECTIONS Mi Vami is just off Beacon Street on Pleasant Street in Coolidge Corner. From Boston taking Beacon Street, take a right one block before Harvard Street onto Pleasant Street. Mi Vami is on the left side squeezed in between a dry cleaner and a convenience store.

By T: Take the Green Line C train to the Harvard Avenue/Coolidge Corner stop. From there walk one block back toward Boston to Pleasant Street, take a left onto Pleasant Street, and Mi Vami is on the left.

PARKING At night there is ample parking on the street.

CAFE BRAZIL

Cafe Brazil is the quintessential Cheap Date restaurant. It's got everything including a quaint interior, dim lights, great food, and get this . . . live guitar music! I love the food, but I have to admit that it's the music that keeps me coming back. As you've probably already guessed, the food is Brazilian, which is a fine mix of tasty meats and unique vegetables. To start off, try the mandioca frita com linguica ($4) which is a fried cassava root (from yucca plants) and grilled sausage. You can also get this without the meat, but with the banana frita (a particular Brazilian specialty). Another appetizer treat is the canjiquinha ($3), a soup of corn grits with pork and garlic.

For an entrée you should consider splitting something (there is a nominal fee for splitting) because they're a little pricey at $9 to $11. If you like fish, there is a whole array of fish dishes that you probably never knew existed. Moqueca de Camarao ($11) is fresh shrimp stewed in vegetables in a sauce of stewing juices mixed with cassava meal. The beef category is my favorite because you can get the Bife Rolet ($11), which is very thin slices of beef rolled up with cheese and ham, grilled and then simmered with veggies. It's incredible! Whether or not you're a vegetarian, a great choice is the vegetarian plate ($9), a mix of sautéed vegetables with sautéed cabbage, mandioca root and banana.

If you haven't already had it, I would highly recommend ordering a side dish of fried bananas ($3), home-style fried potatoes ($3) or Feijao Tropeiro ($3)—a knockout mix of black beans with cassava, bacon, sausage, eggs and garlic. Cafe Brazil has a fine selection of Brazilian beers and wines, but their non-alcoholic drinks are really special. Try the Sucos Tropicais—I think you can imagine what it is, or Guarana, a Brazilian soda made from small red berries.

If you think the prices are too high, you can enjoy Cafe Brazil at lunch time when the menu is the same, portions slightly smaller and prices much lower. As mentioned above, the music is a great treat, so try to go Wednesday through Sunday to get the benefit of these Latin ballads. Music starts at 7 and goes until about 10 (11 on weekends). Parties of more than four should make reservations on weekends.

ADDRESS 421 Cambridge Street, Allston.

PHONE 789-5980.

HOURS Lunch is served 11:30–4 (until 3 on Sundays). Dinner is served 4–10 (11 on weekends).

PRICES Appetizers: $2–4; Entrées: $9–13; Drinks: $1–5; Desserts: $2.50–3.

DIRECTIONS From Storrow Drive, exit at the Double Tree Hotel and take a left onto Cambridge Street. Follow Cambridge Street through about five lights (pass the Sports Depot on Harvard Avenue on your right) and find Cafe Brazil on the right side of the street.

By T/Bus: Take the Green Line B train to the Harvard Avenue stop. From the exit walk north on Harvard Avenue, pass Brighton Avenue and continue to Cambridge Street. Take a left onto Cambridge Street and find Cafe Brazil half a block up on the right side. If you don't want to walk, the 66 Bus will take you from the T stop to the corner of Cambridge Street and Harvard Avenue, and you can walk the block from there. Call the MBTA for alternate bus routes.

PARKING There is usually parking along Cambridge Street. You may have to walk a few blocks.

BLUESTONE BISTRO

Probably the chicest restaurant to be found in Brighton, the Bluestone Bistro has become a hot spot for many people on a budget. Prices are very reasonable considering the high quality of the fare. Crowds come in waves; on any given weekend night you can wait five minutes or 45. Earlier is better if you have no patience with lines. If waiting is really out of the question, you can have a take-out dinner and even get delivery to certain areas.

The Bluestone's fare is a flavorful 90s Italian rendition. Appetizers ($1–7) are diverse and quite filling. Try their version of Baked Brie ($6) in a pastry shell and topped with a tangy chutney or the Bruschetta ($3), an Italian classic concoction of their sourdough bread smothered with tomato, basil, fennel and garlic. Entrées ($4–12) like Vegetarian Lasagna, chock-full of peppers, squash, eggplant, spinach and marscapone cheese, give a whole new zing to an old standby. Other pasta dishes combine tasty, fresh ingredients with some more nouveau additions like sun-dried tomatoes or smoked jalapeno. Since most portions are large, you may want to split a small pizza or appetizer and then share one of Bluestone's large pasta dishes (all pasta dishes are served with a delicious warm sourdough bread).

Pizzas are another good bet, with their choice of whole-wheat or regular crusts, both of which are thick and delicious, and a choice of tomato-basil or regular pizza sauce. You can create your own pizza (sm.: $4, med.: $7, lg.: $11) with a list of 40 different unique toppings including things like artichoke hearts, andouille sausage and feta. They also provide some suggested topping combinations for those who don't trust their own creativity.

For an even cheaper and equally scrumptious entrée, try one of their calzones ($6) filled with five cheeses and then your choice of fillings from Greek, Veggie, Two Sausage, Pesto and Chicken, Italian or Smoked Turkey. Servers are always willing to pack up anything you can't eat, so you can have great leftovers for days to come.

ADDRESS 1799 Commonwealth Avenue, Brighton.

PHONE 254-8309.

PRICES Appetizers: $1–7; Entrées: $4–12; Drinks: $1–4.

HOURS Mon–Thur 5:30–11; Fri 5:30–midnight; Sat 10 a.m.–midnight; Sun 10 a.m.–11 p.m. Brunch served on weekends.

DIRECTIONS The Bluestone Bistro is located on Commonwealth Avenue between Washington Street and Chestnut Hill Avenue and at the corner of Chiswick Street.

By T: The Green Line B train stops across the street from the Bluestone Bistro and provides an easy alternative to parking.

PARKING Street parking is available all around the neighborhood, but spots can be scarce. Patience is the key.

CAFFE LAMPARA

If you want to find one of Boston's best quality Italian restaurants outside the North End, look no further. The food at Caffe Lampara is scrumptious, the service impeccable, the atmosphere is hip (if not trippy) and yet the prices remain reasonable. Caffe Lampara is not your typical Italian "chicken parmesan with a side of spaghetti" place. The food here is more authentic than you will find in many of the restaurants in the North End. At Lampara (Italian for "lightning"), the fare is a mixture of fine meat, chicken and fish cuts with good quality pasta and handfuls of different delicacies like calamari, artichokes, sun-dried tomatoes, portobello mushrooms and polenta. The combinations are unique and almost always successful. Their array of pizzas is also original and tasty: choose from a wide variety of pizzas like Scamorza (smoked mozzarella, roasted eggplant, basil and plum tomatoes) or Make Your Own with 24 different toppings.

A quintessential Cheap Date element here at Caffe Lampara is the large and small sizes of pastas and pizzas. The best way to get a variety of tastes for your palate, and to give your wallet a rest, is to order a couple of small dishes and split them up. This way you can help yourself to more than one of Caffe Lampara's delicious meals. Another great aspect to Caffe Lampara—it's the one place where the "don't fill up on bread" rule doesn't hold. The fresh Italian breads doused with fine olive oils are incredible, and they will bring you more upon request.

Despite how enamored I am of Caffe Lampara's atmosphere, if the total price (drinks can be a bit costly) is out of your budget, I would highly recommend the take-out. This is some of the best take-out in Boston. For about $15 you can get two main dishes, including generous portions of their delicious bread (for added insurance, ask for it). Oh, and did I mention that delivery is *FREE* to a limited area? From where else can you have Cavatappi con Pollo e Carciofi delivered right to your doorstep?

Since Lampara is right on the Green Line B train, you can hop on and be in downtown Boston in minutes.

ADDRESS 916 Commonwealth Avenue, Boston.

PHONE 566-0300. Takeout: 566-7929.

PRICES Appetizers: $2–10; Entrées: $5–17; Drinks: $1–6.

HOURS Mon–Thur 11:30–11; Fri & Sat open until 11:30; Sun 12–10.

DIRECTIONS Located right on Commonwealth Avenue on the Brookline/Boston line, Caffe Lampara is next door to CVS at St. Paul Street, across from the BU Armory.

By T: The T is the easiest way to get there. Take the Green Line B train to the St. Paul Street stop. Lampara is across the street.

PARKING Though Caffe Lampara has valet parking, this is not suggested. With some patience parking can be found on side streets or on Commonwealth Avenue. Try St. Paul Street or Pleasant Street.

NEWBURY COLLEGE

I cannot stress enough what a huge treat a night out at the Newbury College's Mitton House is. Newbury College is a culinary arts school where students not only learn the art of fine cuisine from famous masters, but they also go to school for maître d'hôtel instruction, table waiting and even ice sculpture. The only problem is that these students need somebody to try all their training on.

Enter Cheap Dater.

Here's what you do: Call Newbury College and make a reservation (it may be a couple of weeks, so call now). Then get all dolled up, go out to Brookline to the gorgeous George Mitton House at Newbury College and have one of the best, most elegant meals of your life! Because the entire staff is schooled in serving you, you will be treated like a king and queen. The menu changes, but each meal consists of four courses. The price including everything is $10 per person for lunch and $20 for dinner. Keep in mind that, although they don't serve alcohol, you can bring your own wine and it will be served to you like the finest bottle of Dom Perignon (don't bother bringing hard alcohol or beer because they aren't allowed to serve it).

The whole experience is a dream come true!

ADDRESS 129 Fisher Avenue, Newbury College, Brookline.

PHONE 730-7037.

HOURS Lunch is served Mon–Thur and Sat at noon. Dinner is served Mon–Thur at 6 p.m. These are the only times meals are served.

PRICES Lunch: $10 per person; Dinner: $20 per person. All meals are complete.

DIRECTIONS From Beacon Street go to Cleveland Circle and take a left onto Chestnut Hill Avenue. Take a left on Dean Road, then a right onto Fisher Avenue. Go up Fisher Avenue to find Newbury College at the crest of the hill, and the Mitton House on the left side.

By T: Take the Green Line D train to the Reservoir stop. From there take an inexpensive cab to the top of Fisher Avenue. The 51 and 86 Buses also go to Cleveland Circle.

PARKING There is parking at the college.

CENTRE STREET CAFE

If you live in Jamaica Plain (or JP as the locals refer to it), you probably frequent the Centre Street Cafe already, but if you don't live nearby, it is worth the trip. The menu is extremely colorful and diverse with dishes from all over the world. Guided by the chef and owner Felicia Sanchez, the staff works extremely hard to make your dining experience a comfortable one, despite the small interior and eight available tables. Appetizers ($3–7) are a must with choices such as a pile of divine bruschetta bellissima or polenta paradiso. Salads ($4–6) are also celestial. Try the pear walnut or the Szechwan shaboom salads (I suggest splitting one as an appetizer). Moving on to entrées ($4–13), daily specials, written on the board, are a treat—choose from fish, pasta, quesadillas and a host of other choices. However, the real bargains are the menu entrées:

sesame peanut noodles, smoked bluefish cake plate, South American stir-fry — all around $6. Many of these entrées can be "beefed up" by adding your choice of tofu, chicken or shrimp for a few extra dollars.

Although there are no alcoholic drinks, the drink menu is still quite intoxicating: with blends of fruits and other flavors, they serve up a variety of daily drink specials plus you can BYOB. Although I usually encourage pursuing a different place for dessert—and Jamaica Plain has a fine selection of dessert spots—Centre Street Cafe does serve some excellent sweets. Key lime pie, fudge walnut brownie, and chocolate mousse pie are just a few of their delicacies. If you'd rather take in some of the other neighborhood flavor, try the Coffee Cantata, a few doors down, for dessert and coffee.

Centre Street Cafe also serves a bargain of a brunch ($4–7) on weekends. There's the basic brunch of eggs, toast and all the other good stuff, Mexican morning burritos, and the truckstop breakfast that gives you just about everything you can imagine for $6.

ADDRESS 597 Centre Street, Jamaica Plain.

PHONE 524-9217.

HOURS Dinner is served 5–10. Brunch is available 9–3 on Saturday and Sundays.

PRICES Appetizers $3–5; Entrées: $4–13; Brunch: $4–7.

DIRECTIONS From Huntington Avenue, take a left onto South Huntington Avenue and follow to Centre Street. Pass the Acapulco on your left and follow for about another mile to find the tiny Centre Street Cafe sign on the right side of the street.

By T/Bus: You can take the Green Line E train to the last stop and then walk up Centre Street for about 20 minutes, but it's not a great place to be walking. The best choice is to take the 39 Bus from Copley Square to the Pond Street stop.

PARKING Parking is available on Centre Street and surrounding streets.

COFFEE CANTATA

Much different from its neighbor, Centre Street Cafe, Coffee Cantata specializes in more refined Italian cuisine at varied prices. The interior is small (seems to be the norm in JP), but beautiful with faux crack-painted walls and little Italian details all over. Entrées ($8–14) are a bit pricey, but consist of raviolis with plenty of stuffing, chicken breast Provençal and gnocchi. To keep the cost low, you can choose from an array of sandwiches and pizzas ($4–8) on focaccio with good stuff like mesquite turkey and honey-cured smoked ham, then topped with lots of yummy tidbits and herbs. My favorite part about Coffee Cantata (after the glorious surroundings) is the desserts and coffee drinks. Instead of just reading off the menu for desserts, you can peer into the glass case and choose one of their tasty pastries, cakes, mousses, et al ($1–4). Cheesecake is my favorite, but you may lean toward the tarts and fresh fruits. Non-alcoholic drinks are also rather exotic—they even have an excellent rootbeer, fruity concoctions and Coca-Cola in bottles!

ADDRESS 605 Centre Street, Jamaica Plain.

PHONE 522-2223.

HOURS Mon–Fri 7:30 a.m.–10 p.m. Saturdays open at 8:30 a.m. and Sundays open 9–6.

PRICES Appetizers: $2–7; Entrées: $8–14; Pizzas and sandwiches: ($4–8); Desserts: ($1–4).

DIRECTIONS See directions for the Centre Street Cafe and find Coffee Cantata on the corner of the same block of Centre Street.

By T/Bus: See Centre Street Cafe.

PARKING See Centre Street Cafe.

THE FIVE SEASONS

Not to be confused with the outrageously priced Four Seasons, the Five Seasons is located smack dab in the middle of Jamaica Plain and features all vegetarian specialties. Choose from a large selection of appetizers ($4–6) like grilled shrimp teriyaki, hummus with homemade poppyseed crackers or onion rings served with homemade catsup. Tempura (batter-dipped and deep-fried organic vegetables) and noodles (pan-fried or in broth) ($8–13) are great as entrées and are served with wonderful organic vegetables, seafood (always fresh) or tofu. The house specialties ($9–14) are a bit more money, but are quite large and display some of the Five Seasons' excellent culinary style. The Mexican Delight is a treat with spicy black bean enchiladas, guacamole and organic brown rice with homemade corn chip. Szechuan-style tofu is spicy and silken, served with a mound of Chinese vegetables.

Make sure not to ignore the side dishes ($1–4) so you can enjoy some of their sourdough whole-wheat bread or homemade pickles. Salads are equally worthy—the house salad is a far cry from the norm, with tons of red cabbage, romaine lettuce, watercress and more. Sea salad is a great bargain: for $4 you get the house salad topped with the chilled sea vegetable of the day. You can choose from the savory miso or green goddess dressing—both of which make the meal.

One of the few restaurants in Jamaica Plain to serve beer and wine, the Five Seasons has only organic wine as well as Sam Adams beer. Their fresh squeezed juices are wonderful and a perfect ending to a meal. If you're in the mood for a more substantial sweet, try JP Licks across the street, or check out Coffee Cantata a few blocks back toward South Huntington Avenue on Centre Street for some excellent choices in the decadence category.

ADDRESS 669A Centre Street, Jamaica Plain.

PHONE 524–9016.

HOURS Open for dinner Tue–Sun 4–10; Mon 5–10. Lunch is served Tue–Sat noon–4 and Sun brunch is 10–2.

PRICES Appetizers: $4–6; Entrées: $8–14; Drinks: $1–4.

DIRECTIONS Follow directions to Centre Street Cafe, continue on Centre Street for about three more blocks to find Five Season on your right side.

By bus: Take the 39 Bus from the Back Bay station to Jamaica Plain Center.

PARKING Plenty of street parking is available in Jamaica Plain.

BELLA LUNA

I think colorful is the best way to describe just about everything at Bella Luna, from the menu to the interior and including the staff and clientele. Pizzas are their specialty, as they should be since they're so cheap, unique, and definitely generous. There are three different sizes 8" ($4–9), 12" ($6–13) and the giant 16"($8–18). You can "create your own galactic pie" (there's some kind of outerspace theme in their menu) choosing from over 40 different toppings like shitake mushrooms, bananas, snow peas, roasted garlic, caramelized onions, bamboo shoots, shrimp and about 35 others. If this creates too much havoc in your mind, there are 23 pizza concoctions that will put your mind at ease. Try sol de Cancun with ground beef, hot salsa, onion, jalepeno peppers, cheddar cheese and special seasonings, or the pizza Menino with pepperoni, Italian sausage, mushrooms, peppers, onions and a whole lotta cheese. My favorite is the City Year Pizza—it's "very inclusive" with black olives, ricotta, roasted red peppers, and cheddar cheese. If you prefer the tidiness of a calzone, any of the pizzas can be made into calzones.

Other than pizzas, Bella Luna makes a fantastic salad ($3–8) in both small and family sizes. The sandwiches are hard to resist because you have a choice of French bread or baked-to-order Syrian bread. I would suggest the Syrian because it's piping hot and turns any sandwich into a woufwatering wasterwiece . . . sorry, but I started to drool. If you're at Bella Luna for dinner, you can also order one of the pastas ($8–9) which includes the lasagna of the day (ask about the green lasagna), lemon cilantro chicken over pasta or chicken and broccoli with sun-dried tomatoes and artichoke hearts in a garlic, white wine sauce . . . bella indeeda!

Another plus to Bella Luna is that they have live music Sunday–Thursday nights starting at 8:30. It's worth planning your visit on one of those nights so you can enjoy the free music as well as the good fare. Bella Luna also serves a variety of beers and wines, as well as some excellent desserts ($3–4). I can't praise the magnificent seven chocolate cake enough!

ADDRESS 405 Centre Street, Jamaica Plain.

PHONE 524-6060.

HOURS 11–11 daily. Live music is Sunday to Thursday starting at 8:30.

PRICES Salads: $3–8; Appetizers: $3–4; Pizzas: $4–18 (8" to 16") Sandwiches: $4–6; Pastas: $8–9; Drinks: $1–4; Desserts: $3–4.

DIRECTIONS From Huntington Avenue, take a left onto South Huntington Avenue and follow to Centre Street. At the intersection with Centre Street, bear **left** onto Centre Street.

By T/Bus: You can take the Green Line E train to Heath Street, but the 39 Bus from Copley Square is your best bet. From the Christies stop on the bus, take a **left** onto Centre Street to find Bella Luna a few blocks up on your left.

PARKING Parking is ample on the streets.

DOYLE'S

Open since 1882, Doyle's has weathered war, poverty and Prohibition unscathed. In fact, it has remained a standard of excellence in Jamaica Plain for over a century. Yet a few minutes within will reveal that people far and wide migrate to this authentic watering hole and eatery. At first glance the fare appears somewhat predicable, with potato skins, burgers and sandwiches. But this predictability soon evaporates. Nachos are abundant, light and crispy with tons of freshly chopped vegetables ($5)—share them! Burger plates are packed with delicious additions (from $3). A large pizza starts at $6. To further combat predictability, Doyle's has loads of daily specials that are equally thrifty: boneless prime rib ($10); tomato basil quiche and salad ($3.25); and broiled rainbow trout ($6). Amazing! It's like they're giving away food!

Beers are what draw many people to Doyle's. There are tons of draught beers ($1.50–4) that are always cold and cheap. It's a great place to hang out for a couple of drinks, some dinner and interesting conversation.

ADDRESS 3484 Washington Street, Jamaica Plain.

PHONE 524-2345.

HOURS Open everyday 9–11:30, bar closes at 12:30.

PRICES Appetizers: $2–5; Entrées: $3–12; Beers are very reasonable, $1.50–4.

DIRECTIONS Directions depend on from whence you come. From Boston take Route 1 (the Jamaicaway) to the intersection with Route 203 at the Arborway Rotary. Take a right off the rotary onto Route 203, past the Arnold Arboretum on the right, following the signs to Dorchester. Exit just before the Forest Hills overpass. Turn left at the bottom of the exit ramp. Take the first right, then the first left onto Washington Street. Doyle's is three blocks down on the right at the corner of Williams Street.

By T: Take the Orange Line to Forest Hills. Walk down the steps toward the bus kiosk and turn left onto Washington Street. Walk past the Arborway bus stop on the right and continue down Washington Street for three blocks. Doyle's is on the right, at the corner of Washington and Williams streets. *DON'T WALK ALONE!*

PARKING Doyle's has plenty of parking behind the restaurant.

ANGELO PIZZERIA

You've probably already heard of Santarpio's Pizzeria near the airport in East Boston. Let me tell you, next time you're going to Santarpio's, just keep on going and head over to Angelo's a block away. Although they've only been open for a couple of years, Angelo and Mama Rosa have been making excellent Italian food for decades—and it's paid off because this is some of Boston's very finest.

The interior is a slightly cramped, but you'll understand why when you meet Angelo and his family. There are about seven tables with pictures of Italy covering the walls, and there is a homey charm that abounds from the family that treats you like one of their own. Then there is the food: everything is made fresh every day and made to order (you'd be surprised at how few restaurants do the same!). Your food can sometimes take a while, but this is only because it's made so fresh and delicious that it takes a little more time than other places.

The most difficult thing about Angelo's is deciding what to eat. You should start with an appetizer like the Antipasto Italiano ($7) or the marinated eggplant, provolone, roasted peppers and prosciutto ($6). Then think about ordering one of their excellent pizzas with fresh ingredients instead of the yucky old canned stuff. There are basic pizzas ($6–10) and the gourmet pizzas ($8–14)—both with many merits. If you're in for the gourmet pizza, you're going to have a hard time choosing from the Puttanesca (black olives, artichoke hearts, garlic and capers), the Jo-Jo Special (spinach, garlic, homemade sausage, and white olive oil—extra special because Jo-Jo is Angelo's son) or the Pizza Mista (prosciutto, mushroom, eggplant and artichoke each on its separate quarter of pizza—it's like a great sampler); not to mention about eight other choices. Did I mention that a slice of basic cheese is only a buck?

Keep in mind, though, that the pastas are even better than the pizzas. Mama Rosa makes her ravioli fresh every morning and packs 'em full of fluffy ricotta cheese . . . mmm! There is usually a pasta special each day that comes with salad and a soup for only about $6. Wow! Other pastas ($6–9) also come with salad, bread and butter and serve up a great meal with plenty of leftovers to take home. How about some Chicken or Veal Valdostano ($7) with prosciutto in a cream sauce? Or, homemade cavatelli with sausage ($6.50) and shrimp scampi served over linguine ($8.50). It doesn't stop there. If you are ever so brave that you want to experience a real Italian tradition, go on a Friday or Saturday and order the tripe ($5.75) or stuffed calamari ($7.50).

You can also choose from a wide variety of hot and cold subs ($3–5) that go way beyond the average hoagie—but why get a sub when they have so many great pastas and pizzas and calzones?

If you find that the decor leaves something to be desired, be assured that it can be altered, since Angelo's is a BYOB joint. Be advised that you should also BYOG (no it doesn't stand for Guido), bring your own glasses, because Angelo's only has paper cups and a fine wine in a paper cup is not the best.

When you go to Angelo's, consider taking the East Boston Ferry from Long Wharf. It'll add a great touch of romance to your date. See page 163 for details.

ADDRESS 88 Chelsea Street, East Boston.

PHONE 567-3806.

HOURS Mon–Sat 11–11. Closed Sundays!

PRICES Appetizers: $3–7; Subs: $3–5; Pizzas: $6–10; Pastas: $7–9; Sodas and espresso: $1.

DIRECTIONS From Boston take the Callahan Tunnel and take an immediate right out of the tunnel toward the sign for Santarpio's Pizza. At the light take a right to find Angelo's a few blocks up on the right side.

By T: Take the Blue Line to Maverick station. From the exit walk north to Chelsea Street and follow it about three blocks to find Angelo's on the left side of the street.

PARKING There is usually two-hour parking available on the street.

ANDROS DINER

Nestled in a little wooded area near beautiful McLean Hospital in Belmont, Andros Diner takes diner food to a whole new high. I have always been a fan of diner food, although many feel that it usually leaves something to be desired; not the case at Andros. Not only do they have that campy charm normal to diners, but they specialize in delicious Greek cuisine and let you bring your own booze.

Owned and run by the Andros family, this diner not only specializes in divine Greek cuisine, but the service is always friendly, prices are cheap, and portions are hearty. Although Andros serves the basic diner fare (burgers, grilled cheese and fries), the Greek food is by far the best choice. Daily specials are always a treat, but the mousaka ($6) is out of this world, as is the gyros-n-pita ($5) of lamb as well as chicken and vegetable (here's a little bonus for you: gyros is pronounced "yeeros"—now you don't have to be too embarrassed to order it).

Other successes at Andros Diner include the seafood. Andros Diner will sauté, deep fry and broil their delectable cuts of haddock, sole, bluefish and scallops—all served to order. Naturally, the seafood dishes are the more expensive items on the menu, but even these only start at $5 and go to $10.

Another huge asset of Andros Diner is their breakfast service. It's not fancy, there's no live jazz, just good old fashioned home-cooked breakfast. From 6 to 11 in the morning you can get just about any breakfast for only $1 to $4.25. We're talking eggs, waffles, French toast, bacon, sausage, hot and cold cereals—as far as I can tell, there's nothing too Greek here. Best of all is the Breakfast Special: for $.99 (that ain't no misprint) you can get two eggs, toast and home fries with coffee. I don't think you'll find this anywhere else in Boston.

If you like the sound of Andros Diner but don't often find yourself in Belmont, I will highly suggest a venture out there to experience a little of Greece. Also, while in the neighborhood, see what's playing at the fabulous Belmont Cinema (cheap tickets), or go on a nature walk in some of the surrounding woods. It's worth the trip.

ADDRESS 628 Trapelo Road, Belmont.

PHONE 484-7322.

HOURS Mon 6 a.m.–8 p.m.; Tue–Sat 6–9; Sun 7–1:30 p.m.

PRICES Appetizers: $1–5; Entrées: $5–12; Drinks: $1–3.

DIRECTIONS From Memorial Drive, take Mt. Auburn Street away from Cambridge, then bear right onto Belmont Street (at Star Market). Belmont Street will turn into Trapelo Road. Follow Trapelo Road all the way through Waverly Square (pass a second Star Market on your right side) to find Andros Diner on your left about a half a mile outside of Waverly Square.

By T/Bus: Take the Red Line to the Harvard Square station. From there take the 73 Bus to Waverly Square. Walk five minutes farther down Trapelo Road to find Andros Diner on your left.

PARKING There is parking on both sides of the street, and it's free. Don't you love the suburbs!

DALI RESTAURANT & TAPAS BAR

This is one of my publisher's favorite places. He tells me that this is the way all restaurants should be—packed with interesting people, filled with conversation and loud laughter, decorated with everything from peonies to panties, committed to great food and good times, and hosted by Tamara and Mario who obviously love their restaurant and who spend time to make their diners feel welcome.

Not everyone would put Dali in the category of "cheap." Tapas are priced between $4 and $8. Entrées cost between $15 and $20.

From the point of view of simple taste, those of us with ample folding money will consider the food a great value for the experience. But this is a restaurant where knowing how to order the a meal and sharing with your date can make all the difference in the world.

If you share your tapas and an entrée and have a bottle of Spanish wine your bill shouldn't come to more than $50 plus tax and tip. Now that's not too bad.

The wait staff is used to people sharing and they readily will bring extra plates and silverware.

I suggest you start with three tapas. I like the hot tapas best. For instance, try the *Queso de Cabra*, (goat cheese), the *Setas* (meaty mushrooms cooked in garlic) and the *Chipirones Rellenos* (stuffed squid in its own ink)—all are around $5 apiece. Don't worry there are plenty of other tapas, both hot and cold, from which to choose.

For your entrée try Dali's *Pescado a la Sal* (sea bass baked in rock salt). There's plenty for two and dish is presented wonderfully. Another recommended entrée is the Cor*dero Asado* (roasted lamb). Both entrées are $18–19 (thats only $9–9.50 per person when sharing).

To accompany your meal select one of the Spanish wines from Dali's wine list. The inexpensive wines are plenty good. For a red wine you might try the Peñascal (around $15) or a Rioja such as Faustino VII (also around $15). You can't go wrong with the wine list. Incidentally, I've been told that Dali Restaurant pours more Spanish wine than any other restaurant in the United States.

If it's your birthday (or your date's), this is a great restaurant to choose for your celebration. Dali will help you out with singing accompanied with candles and bubbles.

If you are a person who loves life, you'll have a blast at Dali. Eating out doesn't get much more romantic or fun than this.

ADDRESS 415 Washington Street, Somerville (on the Cambridge-Somerville line).

PHONE 661-3254.

HOURS Every evening 5:30–11.

PRICES Tapas: $4–7.50; Entrées: $15–20; Drinks: Wine by the glass is between $3.50 and $5.50, and Sangria is $9 a liter.

DIRECTIONS On the corner of Washington Street and Beacon Street in Somerville. If you are coming from Inman Square take Hampshire Street (it turns into Beacon in Somerville). You will see Dali on your left. From Harvard go down Kirkland Street (it will turn into Washington Street in Somerville).

By T/Bus: There isn't a really close T station. The closest stop is Harvard Square on the Red Line. From the T exit walk across Harvard Yard to Kirkland Street. Turn right and walk down Kirkland to Dali Restaurant. It should be about a 20-minute walk. If you can figure out the bus system, there is a bus that runs up Hampshire/ Beacon Streets from Boston to Porter Square.

PARKING Park on the street. It's not too bad, especially in Somerville. Cambridge is almost impossible with all the "resident only" spaces. Don't park in the private parking lot across Beacon street. You may get towed.

BEER AND BREWERY TOURS

It used to be that you could hardly find a beer in Boston any better than Budweiser, but in recent years Boston has become a great mecca for beer lovers, with microbreweries popping up faster than political scandals. What does all this mean for you? This means that not only can you tour some of these flavorful facilities, but you can also taste all these suds for *FREE*! The following is a list of a few of Boston's best breweries. Each will take you on a tour of their factory showing you exactly how beer goes from hops to glass, and then they will give you a little beer tasting (provided you are 21). Tour times and locations seem to change frequently, so call ahead to get brochures and information.

MASS BAY BREWING COMPANY 306 Northern Avenue (Pier 4), Boston 574-9551

The age of the microbrewery in Boston started with Harpoon Ale and the Mass Bay Brewing Company. Three guys at Harvard Business School who really liked beer decided that they would put their heads together, come up with a the perfect ale and start their own company. (The Mass Bay Brewing Company's other claim to fame is that they used to employ the author—I was the only high-school girl who worked in a brewery.) Factory tours are given on Fridays and Saturdays at 1 p.m. and are *FREE*. You can get a tour of the facility and then taste their fabulous suds. Another bonus is their "Harpoon 5:30 Club" on Tuesdays, Wednesdays or Thursdays, when you can get together a group of people to have your own private tour and tasting. Call ahead for details. Mass Bay Brewing Company is also host to a number of awesome parties throughout the year. Call and ask to get put on their mailing list so you can get invitations to the fun!

BOSTON BEER COMPANY 30 Germania Street, Jamaica Plain 522-9080

Makers of Samuel Adams beers, ales, etc., these guys even have a whole museum dedicated to the art of brewing and the history of Sam Adams. Tours are given Thursdays and Fridays at 2 p.m. and Saturdays at noon, 1 and 2 p.m. Yes—samples are given, and the cost is only $1!

Samuel Adams also has a brew house open in Copley Square at 710 Boylston Street where you can do more than just taste their products.

ATLANTIC COAST BREWERY 50 Terminal Street, Boston 242-6464

Makers of one of my all-time favorite beers, Tremont Ale, the Atlantic Coast Brewery will give tours of their facility whenever you want. I like that on-demand quality in a business. Call to set up an appointment so you can taste their ale and become a convert like me.

In addition to factory tours, you can also experience beer making at its best at one of the many microbrewery restaurants in Boston. Here you can sample some of the finest beers in New England in the comfort of a restaurant. A couple of brew houses are listed here below to get you started. In terms of restaurants, these aren't exactly the cheapest, so I can't necessarily recommend them for eating—but if you stick to burgers, it will be pretty reasonable.

BOSTON BEER WORKS 61 Brookline Avenue, Fenway 536-2337

This place gets very crowded during Red Sox season, so you'll do better to stay away then. If you want to play some pool afterwards, there are a couple of good places like Jillian's and Boston Billiards, although they're rather expensive. (A little Cheap Dates secret is that Aku Aku, down Brookline Avenue, has two pool tables that are just $1 per game. Can't get that at the other places! Just don't tell too many people.)

CAMBRIDGE BREWING COMPANY 1 Kendall Square, Cambridge 494-1994.

This is located in a little mall area with a few other fun places, and after experiencing the brews, you can play some pool at Flat Top Johnny's. It's more expensive than Aku Aku, but cheaper than the rest.

THE COMMONWEALTH BREWING COMPANY 138 Portland Street, Boston 523-8383 (near the Fleet Center)

Just as Boston Beer Works, the Commonwealth Brewing Company gets really crowded when there's something going on at the Fleet Center. (Do you see a pattern emerging between the proximity of brew houses, sports facilities and pool tables?) The best part of the Commonwealth Brewing Company is that they give tours of their basement brewing facilities so you get the best of both worlds: see how the beer is made, then hang out and drink deeply. Tours are generally given at noon and 4 p.m.

JOHN HARVARD'S BREW HOUSE 33 Dunster Street, Harvard Square 868-3585

I once fell in love at John Harvard's Brew House in Harvard Square. I'm not sure how much can be attributed to the beer, but it will always hold a special place in my heart. Even if it doesn't in yours, it should hold a special place in your beer drinking agenda. The interior has some really funky stained-glass windows, and not too many Harvard students. An added bonus is the live music played on Monday and Tuesday nights. Check it out with someone you like a lot; maybe you too will fall in love!

EATING ALTERNATIVES

No, this section does not include tips like diet pills and Slim Fast shakes instead of meals. Rather, by eating alternatives, I am referring to the many creative ways of sharing a meal together without actually going to a restaurant (and subsequently saving some dough!). Don't get me wrong! I love eating out. But sometimes a change of scenery is a great way to spice up a date. Here you will find a few alternatives to the same old dinner date.

PICNICS

I understand that the testy weather of Boston makes picnicking an unreliable option, but there are plenty of perfect picnic days in 365 days a year.

The main attraction of picnicking for myself is the surroundings (I bet you thought I was going to say the price!). Boston is packed with perfect picnic places, many of which go unused. I usually use picnics to clean out my refrigerator and pack all those yummy leftovers. It's called *SECOND DAY SMORGASBORD*. It's great! You get a taste of everything great, there's no preparation needed and you're cleaning at the same time. I usually pack a little vino, a big blanket, some reading material which never gets touched, and some bug spray. The following is a list of just of few picks of Boston's fine picnicking possibilities.

- Harvard Yard
- Esplanade
- Larz Anderson Park
- Public Garden
- MFA Courtyard
- Walden Pond
- The Fens
- Crystal Lake
- Brookline Reservoir
- Riverway
- Jamaica Pond
- Fisher Park
- North End Beach
- Charles Embankment
- Gardner Museum Yard
- Charlesbank Park

And the list goes on, but I think you get the picture. If not, the picture looks something like this: You and your date with a fantastic picnic surrounded by the gorgeous scenery of Boston. No waiter to tip, no costly entrées or expensive wine list from which to choose.

"Fine. Picnics are great, but what if the weather is bad??"
You'll see!

COOKING

Yes, I've said it. The C word. Oh, really! Stop cowering. Cooking is not that hard. Honest. But what makes cooking such a cool option is the prospect of the two of you cooking together. It's not making music, but it's close enough. To really get to know a person you want to see all aspects of them, right? Well, seeing how the two of you work together is a major part of that discovery. I think it's also a good idea to establish a pattern early on of the two of you preparing meals, instead of getting into the rut of one person always cooking while the other watches the news in another room. Studies show (no I'm *NOT* making this up!) that the biggest problem with most relationships is a lack of talking. People don't take the time out to see what's going on with their partner. While cooking together, you can discuss how your day went, what's new at work, plans you want to make. I must admit, though, that my favorite part of cooking together is that it gets done twice as fast, and you'll be eating in no time.

If you don't know what to make, there are plenty of cook-books out there at all levels that have tons of great ideas. Investing a couple of bucks in a good cookbook will save you hundreds of dollars in idle restaurant meals. Try it once and see how it goes. If it's a major flop, then next time call for take-out!

TAKE-OUT

Take-out seems like a pretty obvious solution, but most people consider take-out only an option when sitting around watching the Super Bowl or repainting the apartment. The truth is, take-out is a fantastic idea whenever you want professional food without the expensive environment. Also, it is worth mentioning that almost every restaurant does take-out these days. From lobster to cheese-burgers, you can find it on take-out menus. So the next hurdle is *WHERE TO EAT TAKE-OUT*. That's easy.

Remember: The world is your oyster—okay, maybe just Boston—and in this case you can even eat the oyster. Make sense? Maybe not, but the point is that you can combine take-out with a picnic and go anywhere with dinner in your hand and make some beautiful spots your dining room. One of my favorites is to go to Larz Anderson Park and sit and watch the sunset while noshing on La Famiglia pasta. If weather or imagination are a problem, there is always your home. Personally, I don't think that it's against the rules to secretly bring take-out home and then play it off as your own, just like Holly Hunter in the movie *Always*. But if deception is not your forte, realize that your date would probably rather have a delicious meal made by a stranger than charred pasta from you.

ALPHABETICAL RESTAURANT LIST

EXPLORING BOSTON
HISTORIC BOSTON
HARBOR CRUISES
AUCTIONS
MUSEUMS
LIBRARIES
OUTDOOR ACTIVITIES

HISTORIC BOSTON

You may wonder why I included a section on **Historic Boston** in a book about dating. But I think you will be surprised to discover how romantic a historic date can be. For one thing, exploring together the history of Boston gives you an opportunity to get to know your date in a unique forum. By learning together the history of Boston and seeing these beautiful sites, you will create a special kind of intimacy that is often lost during other dates. And, you may also be surprised at how romantic Boston's history really is with its amorous vistas from ancient buildings, intriguing graveyards and sultry sites that hold the city's 300-year history. Much of America's history and literature has had Boston as its setting; by visiting these spots, you are setting your own stage for drama, intrigue and courtship.

THE FREEDOM TRAIL

A chapter on **Historic Boston** would ne'er be complete without the Freedom Trail. It's a great way to take a crash course in Boston's history. The beauty of the Freedom Trail is that you can do the entire three-mile trail in one day by diligently following the red-painted lines on the street, or you can take your time and do sections of it, enjoying each neighborhood to its fullest. There is no real beginning or ending to the Freedom Trail's red-painted or red-brick line on the sidewalk, but most people begin at either Boston Common or the Charlestown Navy Yard. If you are driving, it's best to start at Charlestown Navy Yard because there is free parking. Either way, you should begin with a good guide. The Boston National Historical Park Visitor Center at 5 State Street (across from the Old State House) gives *FREE* tours in summer, and on weekends in the fall and spring. Taking one of these group tours is a great idea if you really want to get the word on Boston's past. Guides are informative and amusing. If it's your first time doing the Freedom Trail, this is probably the smartest choice. If you feel that you can't commit to a group tour like this, you're better off getting a printed guide and following it at your own pace. This is my preference—and it's a little more romantic for a date.

Although you can stop anywhere on the way for a snack or meal, the North End is not only a fantastic neighborhood for food, but it will be a good stopping place to regain some energy for the rest of the trip.

There are 16 official stops on the Freedom Trail, but this doesn't do justice to the hundreds of other niches and details that should be absorbed. Most of the sites on the trail are buildings that have interesting artifacts on the inside too (although some are just outdoor monuments). Most indoor sites are *FREE*, although some have a nominal fee. You don't have to go into these if you don't want to (thus making the experience totally *FREE*), but a couple of minutes inside will help round out your experience. Here is a list of the 16 official sites on the Freedom Trail. An asterisk indicates a fee.

- The State House
- Park Street Church
- Granary Burying Ground
- King's Chapel
- Benjamin Franklin Statue
- Old Corner Bookstore
- Old South Meeting House*
- Old State House*
- Faneuil Hall
- Quincy Market
- Paul Revere House*
- Old North Church
- Copp's Hill Burying Ground
- USS Constitution (and Museum*)
- USS Cassin Young
- Bunker Hill Monument (and Museum)

TRINITY CHURCH

One of Boston's pride and joy pieces of architecture, Trinity Church is also the Hub's largest Episcopal church. But you need not be an Episcopalian to enjoy this Romanesque delight. The interior is extravagant, highly detailed and lavishly decorated with rich, lush colors. One expects to see Cupid float out from the heavenly dome to pierce some hearts.

Sunday tours are somewhat short, but you don't really need a tour guide to make you realize that this is a truly magnificent church. A real treat is to go to the Sunday 11:00 a.m. service, where Trinity's choral group is at its best. After the service, you can stay for the 20-minute tour. A light brunch in Copley Square would be a perfect complement to the morning. Try some of the surrounding cafes, such as Small Planet, or choose one of the many new (and sometimes temporary) spots opening in the area. If the weather is nice, try packing a picnic and enjoying Trinity's environs. Mimosas and strawberries are always amorously appropriate.

Trinity Church offers some of Boston's finest music all year round. Call for a seasonal schedule or stop by and put yourself on their mailing list.

ADDRESS Copley Square.

PHONE 536-0944.

PRICES There is never any admission and Sunday tours are *FREE*.

HOURS Trinity is open daily 8–6. Services are Sundays 8:30, 11 (this is the best one) and 6 p.m. Wednesday services are at 12:10 and 5:30. Call first to make sure.

DIRECTIONS Directly outside the Green Line's Copley stop and near the Orange Line's Back Bay stop, Trinity Church is impossible to miss; across Dartmouth Street and Copley Square from the Boston Public Library.

PARKING Copley Square is flanked with on-street meter parking. Just be patient and willing to walk a few blocks. Bring quarters. Parking on Sunday mornings before the 11 a.m. service is the easiest and it is *FREE*.

CHRISTIAN SCIENCE MOTHER CHURCH

Before I visited the Christian Science Mother Church, the thing I knew about this religion is that when they're sick, they don't go to doctors. Boy, was I an idiot! What I now know is that this is a fascinating religion filled with kind and generous people. But even if you don't have any interest in becoming a Christian Scientist, a trip to their Mother Church will be both edifying and enjoyable.

The enormous dome of the Christian Science Mother Church– the world headquarters of this religion—has adorned Boston for almost a hundred years. One look at it makes you see why this is the Mother Church . . . because this is a *mother dome*. If you think the outside is impressive, wait until you see the inside. The church is home to one of the largest organs in the country; yes, that would be a *mother organ*! There are also dozens of incredible stained-glass windows and other gorgeous features. Tours begin on the hour and last 30 minutes. If you have time to kill before a tour begins, hop over to the Mapparium and start your visit there.

The Mapparium is an enormous *mother globe*, illuminated from behind with a glass bridge that lets you walk through the center and view the world from the inside. Sound weird? It kind of is, but nonetheless, spectacular! The acoustics are amazing–you and your date can be at opposite ends of the world and whisper sweet nothings to each other. Be careful, though, because literally the whole world will hear you.

From my experience here, Christian Scientists are the nicest people and are always willing to answer any questions in the most patient and informative fashion. While you're in the building, make sure to ask about the two lights in the front hall. For more complicated questions on the Christian Science faith, there is an ingenious question board outside of the globe that will tell you what it means to be a Christian Scientist.

After you go through the globe, you can visit the sales room filled with almost every Christian Scientist piece of literature in existence. They will even give you their excellent and well-respected *Christian Science Monitor*, *FREE*. That alone should be reason to go!

ADDRESS 250 Mass. Ave., Boston.

PHONE Visitor Services: 450-3790.

HOURS Church: Mon–Sat 10–4 (with last tour at 3) and Sundays 11:15–2.

Mapparium: Mon–Sat 10–4 *CLOSED MONDAYS*!

PRICES All tours are *FREE*!

DIRECTIONS It's difficult to miss the *mother dome* on Mass. Ave. between Huntington Avenue and Boylston Street near Symphony Hall.

By T: Take the Green Line E train to Symphony Hall and walk towards the Plaza.

PARKING There is special visitor parking underneath the Reflecting Pool. Parking is on a first-come, first-served basis. Get a ticket upon entering and then have it signed by a tour guide or someone in the building. To get to the garage from Mass. Ave., go into the driveway near the Horticultural Hall/Boston Magazine building and follow it around behind the church toward the Reflecting Pool. If this is full, there is meter parking on Huntington Avenue.

THE STATE HOUSE

Although the State House is on the Freedom Trail, this towering golden dome deserves a little more attention. Before it was the towering golden dome, it was the cow pasture of John Hancock. Mr. Bulfinch is the genius architect behind this wonder—it's one of his finest buildings. If you've ever wondered exactly what goes on under that dome, and want to see first-hand the beautiful marble interior and stained-glass skylight, a *FREE* 25-minute tour will satisfy your curiosity. You'll learn much about the way Massachusetts is run, find out how certain phrases and symbols were employed, and see the Hall of Flags with battle flags from the Civil and Spanish-American wars, and from World Wars I and II. Tours are given by informative interns who are friendly and welcome questions.

The entire State House is climate-controlled, making this stop the perfect escape from sweltering summer heat or blustering winter cold. If you cannot get a guided tour (the last leaves at 3:30), the staff will provide you with a short walking guide book. Although the book is a little more detailed in presentation, it isn't nearly as friendly as the live guides.

Before leaving the grounds, check out the Archive Museum which has its own entrance on the side of the State House. Here you can peruse some of the state's oldest and most important documents. When you're done with this, make sure to hit the Boston

Athenaeum and King's Chapel. Or, if you're really in a good mood and wouldn't mind splurging, stop in the Hampshire House (84 Beacon Street) to nurse a $4 drink while looking out over the Public Garden.

ADDRESS The State House is located at the crest of Beacon Hill where Park Street joins Beacon Street.

PHONE 727-3676.

PRICES Admission, guided tours and guide books are *FREE*. (If you are a Taxachusetts resident, you might argue that they aren't really free.)

HOURS Mon-Fri 10-4. Naturally, closed on weekends. Guided tours start every half hour, or when there is someone to guide. Self tours are allowed anytime on weekdays 10-4.

DIRECTIONS At the top of Beacon Hill, the State House is virtually impossible to miss with its golden dome.

By T: Take the Red or Green Line to the Park Street station. Out the exit, look up the hill for the gold dome. A three-minute walk and you'll be standing in front of the State House.

PARKING As with most downtown Boston sites, parking is very difficult. It's best to park at a T stop that has parking and take the T in. But if you're determined, try your hand at on-street parking, or the newly restored parking garage under the Common with an entrance on Charles Street.

NEW OLD SOUTH CHURCH

The Old Old South Church no longer stands, nor does the Old Old Old South Church. What we are left with is the New Old South Church. Make sure not to confuse the New Old South Church with the Old North Church at 193 Salem Street in the North End, nor the Old West Church at 131 Cambridge Street. If you are confused, think of it as the smaller yet equally majestic church in Copley Square.

Once you've deciphered all this, you'll be glad you gave it the effort. No one would want to confuse this beautiful northern Italian gothic church with any other. From the exterior, it's clear that this is a special treat, but often it gets dwarfed by the hugeness of Trinity Church. The colorfully ornamented interior has the lush splendor of Trinity Church, with a cozier charm that will keep you coming back anytime you want to find a little solace from the bustle of Copley Square. It's great to know that after one of those not so cheap strolls down Boylston and Newbury streets, there is always a completely free oasis where you can't be tempted to splurge on something.

Owing to financial difficulties at the Old South Church, there are no guided tours during the week. You'll have to find the fascinating details on your own, or ask the receptionist some questions. If you plan on attending the Sunday service from 11-12 you may be able get a guided tour afterwards. Ask at the reception desk if there will be anyone after the service that could take you around.

The New Old South Church is also host to a few concerts, lectures and recitals. Call and ask for a program for details.

ADDRESS 645 Boylston Street, Copley Square.

PHONE 536-1970.

HOURS Open Mon-Fri 9–5; *CLOSED SATURDAYS* ; Sun 1–3. Services held Sundays at 9 and 11.

PRICES Naturally it's *FREE*, unless you'd like to make a small contribution to ensure that this beautiful church remains functioning.

DIRECTIONS Located on the corner of Boylston and Dartmouth streets across from the Boston Public Library; it's adjacent to the Copley T station.

By T: Take the Green Line to Copley station. Once above ground, you should be standing in front of the New Old South Church.

PARKING It's no fun trying to park in Copley Square. The New

Old South Church is adjacent to the Copley Green Line station, and you will certainly save quarters and steps by taking the T instead of trying to find a spot in this neighborhood. But if you are dead set on driving, I would suggest a few of the side streets in the area, perhaps on Dartmouth Street toward either the South End or the Charles River. Bring quarters and plan to spend 10–20 minutes looking for a spot.

OLMSTED NATIONAL HISTORIC SITE

Frederick Law Olmsted was the greensman who created Boston's beautiful and world-renowned Emerald Necklace. If you don't already know, the Emerald Necklace is the series of parks that extend from the Back Bay Fens to Franklin Park, enhancing Mother Nature's work as they wind along the rivulets of the Charles.

To see into the life of the genius who created the Emerald Necklace (and also New York City's Central Park), you can visit his beautiful historic home that sits upon two acres of gorgeous Brookline land. The site is run by the National Park Service and offers a tour of examples of Olmsted's works.

Olmsted's home makes for a pleasant afternoon outing, and must be accompanied by a stroll around the Brookline Reservoir. (Ask for directions—its only a five-minute walk.) The Brookline Reservoir is by far the prettiest of its kind in the area. You can wander around the reservoir, play Frisbee, or just sit and take in the beauty. To me, the Brookline Reservoir is particularly handsome in the springtime when the cherry blossoms are in full bloom. The Brookline Reservoir is the perfect excuse to pack a picnic lunch and save a few bucks on lunch out.

If you're determined to go out to eat, the Brookline branch of Fajitas & 'Ritas is down Route 9 about two miles toward Boston.

While you're in the area, and if you want to take in more of the lush Brookline sites, try the Larz Anderson Transportation Museum and Park (see page 177).

ADDRESS 99 Warren Street, Brookline.

PHONE 566-1689.

HOURS Fri-Sun 10-4:30. Other days by appointment.

PRICES *FREE*.

DIRECTIONS From Route 9 coming out of Boston, take a left at Warren Street. Follow Warren Street for about two blocks and find the Olmsted site on the corner of Warren and Dudley streets.

By T: Take the Green Line D train to Brookline Hills. From there take a right onto Cypress Street, cross Route 9 and follow Cypress Street to the lights at Walnut Street and take a right. Follow Walnut Street until it ends at Warren Street, take a left and follow Warren Street to the corner of Dudley Street.

PARKING Parking is behind the house and on the street.

JOHN F. KENNEDY NATIONAL HISTORIC SITE

I need not explain who JFK was and continues to be, but did you know that you could visit the house where the former president was born on May 29, 1917? When Kennedy became president, his mother, the late Rose Kennedy, re-bought the house of his birth and donated it to become a historical site. She even redecorated the house to look exactly as it did when the president lived there.

The house is located in the Coolidge Corner section of Brookline, which abounds with fun-filled activities. There are hundreds of shops to peruse (two excellent bookstores—Barnes and Noble and Booksmith), coffee shops where you can read the book you just bought, the Coolidge Corner Cinema (one of Boston's coolest) and plenty of inexpensive restaurants.

A trip to the JFK Historic Site may open up a whole new world for you. You'll get some insight into the life of one of our country's most influential presidents, and you'll get to poke around Coolidge Corner. If you want to get the full JFK experience, you can step into the church where he was baptized. St. Aidan's Church at 158 Pleasant Street (at Freeman Street) is just a hop, skip and a jump from his birthplace. Call 277-0799 for directions and to find out when you can visit this beautiful church. For some great Middle Eastern food in the neighborhood, check out Mi Vami on Pleasant Street. See the *Feasting Boston* chapter for details.

ADDRESS 83 Beals Street, Brookline.

PHONE 566-7937.

HOURS Wed–Sun 10–4:30. Tours are 10:45, 11:45, 1, 2, 3 and 4.

PRICES *FREE*.

DIRECTIONS From Commonwealth Avenue take a left onto Harvard Avenue. At Beals Street take a left and follow the signs to the JFK Historic Site.

By T: You can take either the B or C train of the Green Line to Harvard Avenue. From there you can walk five or six blocks to Beals Street. At Beals Street, follow the signs to the house.

PARKING Parking is available on the street.

THE GIBSON HOUSE

If you have ever had any interest in anything Victorian, the Gibson House should be the next stop on your list. This beautiful Back Bay house is home to the Victorian Society—and it's no wonder; it's filled with original furnishings and decorative arts of the period. A half-hour tour will not only take you through all the gorgeous rooms, fully intact, and tell the story of the Gibson family who lived here from 1859 to 1956, but you will also get a behind-the-scenes look at servants quarters, kitchen and laundry rooms. Glorious high ceilings and rich textures fill this house with beautiful light, color and imagery. It's an extremely romantic date.

When you're done, a stroll through the Public Garden is in order. You can pick up some great sandwiches for a picnic at the Cafe de Paris on Arlington Street between Newbury and Boylston streets. If a sit-down meal is in order, try the Parish Cafe at 361 Boylston Street.

ADDRESS 137 Beacon Street, Back Bay.

PHONE 267-6338.

HOURS Wed–Sun 1–5. Tours are at 1, 2 and 3, May–October. In winter, the Gibson House is open on weekends, 1–5.

PRICES $4.

DIRECTIONS Located on Beacon Street between Arlington and Berkeley streets, The Gibson House is right off Storrow Drive near the Hatch Shell.

By T: Take the Green Line to the Arlington Street station. From the exit walk about five blocks (walking along the Public Garden) to Beacon Street. Take a left onto Beacon Street and walk down half a block to find the Gibson House on the left side.

PARKING Unless you are blessed by the gods, parking is impossible. Occasionally you can find a meter spot on Beacon or Marlborough streets, but it's rare. Take the T.

NICHOLS HOUSE

I love most historic houses, but the Nichols House especially tickles my fancy because it is a private home that is open to the public, giving you the feeling of invited guests. Rooms are decorated in a variety of styles ranging from 15th to the 20th century. A half-hour tour gives you an ample sampling of all the rooms.

Once through here, take a walk down the hill on Mt. Vernon Street to Louisburg Square. This little area of Boston is the quintessential Beacon Hill residence; Senator Kerry and wife Theresa Heinz have just made Louisburg Square their residence. Stroll around and take a peek inside the windows of the homes of people who don't need to go on Cheap Dates!

ADDRESS 55 Mt. Vernon Street, Beacon Hill.

PHONE 227-6993.

HOURS Tues, Thur, Fri and Sat 1–5. Hours often vary. CALL AHEAD!

PRICES $4.

DIRECTIONS From Charles Street take a left onto Mt. Vernon Street, up the hill to find the Nichols House at the peak of the hill on the left side.

By T: Take the Red or Green Line to Park Street station. From the exit walk up Park Street toward the State House, take a left onto Beacon Street, and then a right onto Joy Street. Walk up that hill, and then take a left onto Mt. Vernon Street.

PARKING It's close to impossible to park anywhere in this neighborhood. If you do drive, try around Government Center and Charles Street for a spot, or park at the underground lot at Boston Common (entrance on Charles Street).

JOHN HANCOCK OBSERVATORY

I once had a date begin the evening by skyrocketing me 60 floors in the air. No, he wasn't a pilot, but he did take me to the John Hancock Observatory. It was one of the most romantic starts to a date I have ever had (too bad the rest wasn't as good). Since then, I find myself returning to the Hancock Observatory over and over again. You see, despite having lived in Boston for many years, I still find myself a little turned around in this rambling city of ours. One trip up to the observatory will certainly straighten you out, and be a fantastic accompaniment to any date.

I could list all that you will see, but that would take an entire book. Instead get ready for one spectacular view of Boston from which you and your date can gaze and learn the intricate history of Boston. The observatory has a few exhibits running at all times, and a photo series of overhead color graphics to help decipher what you're looking at. Also there is a little movie room where a film on Boston's history will take you back in time.

Keep in mind that Boston looks very different from day to night. A good way to experience both is to go before sunset, watch the sun dip below the beautiful horizon and then watch the city light up.

ADDRESS 200 Clarendon Street, Back Bay.

PHONE 572-6429.

HOURS Mon–Sat 9 a.m.–11 p.m. Opens at noon on Sundays (10 a.m. May–October).

PRICES Adults: $4.25.

DIRECTIONS From Boylston Street in Copley Square take a right onto Clarendon Street behind Trinity Church. The mirrored Hancock Building is one block up on the right side.

By T: From the Green Line's Copley stop, walk across the Trinity Church park area, pass Trinity Church on your left to find the Hancock right in front of you. From the Orange Line Back Bay station, walk down Dartmouth Street to Stuart Street, take a right and find the Hancock one block down on the right side.

PARKING The best solution to the parking problem in Copley Square is to park in the Copley Place lot after 5 p.m., purchase something for $5 or more and get your ticket validated for free parking all evening. Street parking can be found, but you need a lot of patience.

MOUNT AUBURN CEMETERY

Who would've thought that a cemetery would be this romantic? But trust me, this place is tops in the romantic allure department. Spring and fall are the ideal seasons to take a stroll through the beautiful acreage. Not only is Mt. Auburn a cool cemetery, but it is also a botanical garden and birdwatcher's paradise. Begin your exploration by stopping at the office near the main entrance to pick up a map and guide that will help you identify the graves of all the famous people. The Massachusetts Horticultural Society has worked amazingly hard to make Mt. Auburn Cemetery as gorgeous as it is today. In 1831, the Society established an experimental garden, and to this day the greenhouse is open to the public frequently in the summer (call ahead for details). Even without going to the greenhouse, you can see their handy work at every turn on your stroll; trees and plants are labeled for your convenience. Make sure not to miss climbing the Washington Tower, from which you can get one of the most interesting views of Boston and environs. Unfortunately, picnics, bicycles and dogs are not allowed.

ADDRESS 580 Mt. Auburn Street (Route 16), Cambridge.

PHONE 547-7105.

HOURS Open daily dawn to dusk. The office is open Mon–Sat 8:30–4.

PRICES *FREE*.

DIRECTIONS From Harvard Square take Mt. Auburn Street out of the Square and follow for about three miles to find the cemetery on the left side of the street.

By T/Bus: Go to Harvard station on the Red Line, then a 5-minute bus ride on the 71, 72 or 73 Bus.

PARKING You'll have to find a spot on the street to park your vehicle.

Here are few more suggestions for Historic Boston dates:

> **ARLINGTON STREET UNITARIAN UNIVERSALIST CHURCH** 351 Boylston Street, Back Bay 536-7050.
>
> **BULFINCH PAVILION AND ETHER DOME AT MASS GENERAL HOSPITAL** 55 Fruit Street, Government Center 726-2000.
>
> **CATHEDRAL CHURCH OF ST. PAUL** 138 Tremont Street, Boston 482-5800.
>
> **CHURCH OF THE ADVENT** 30 Briber Street, Beacon Hill 523-2377.

CHURCH OF THE COVENANT 67 Newbury Street, Back Bay 266-7480.

HEADQUARTERS HOUSE (guided tours) 55 Beacon Street, Beacon Hill 742-3190.

HENRY WADSWORTH LONGFELLOW HOUSE 105 Brattle Street, Cambridge 876-4491.

HARRISON GRAY OTIS HOUSE at 131 Cambridge Street, Government Center 227-3956

KING'S CHAPEL 58 Tremont Street, Boston 227-2155.

OLD WEST CHURCH 131 Cambridge Street, Government Center 227-5088.

PARK STREET CHURCH 1 Park Street, Downtown Crossing 523-3383.

SAINT STEPHEN'S CHURCH 24 Clark Street (at Hanover Street), North End 523-1230.

HARBOR CRUISES

For years I never embarked on a harbor cruise because I assumed that it was outrageously expensive like whale watching tours. Luckily someone clued me in. Now harbor cruises are one of my favorite things to do on dates, or even if I just want to get away by myself. There are a number of different companies that have harbor cruise services. When you go on any of the tours, remember that it gets pretty chilly out there even in the dead heat of summer. Bring warm clothes, binoculars, lunches and especially sunscreen—no matter what time of year! Most of the cruise companies run their cruises from early May to late October. I have been perfectly satisfied with the cruises done by BAY STATE CRUISE COMPANY (723-7800). They provide four great and reasonably priced tours that all leave from Long Wharf at the Marriott Long Wharf Hotel (Prices are subject to change):

Inner Harbor: $5

A 55-minute, narrated tour of the inner part of Boston Harbor from the Freedom Trail to Logan Airport. There is an option to get off at Charlestown Navy Yard, checking out the USS Constitution, and then catching a later cruise back to Long Wharf.

Outer Harbor Cruise: $7

This 90-minute cruise will take you out among some of Boston's many harbor islands. Here again you can get off at George's Island and explore old Fort Warren. Bring a picnic and a blanket, or hike around until you want to go home, and then catch another cruise back to Long Wharf. There is a *FREE* Water Taxi from George's Island to some of the smaller islands in summer time. Call for schedules.

Sunset Cruises: $7

This is one of my favorites because it can be the beginning to a great evening date! There are drinks available on board (very expensive drinks!), and you can sit and watch the sunset reflect off Boston's beautiful architecture. These cruises last about an hour and a half. It's a class act way to begin an evening!

Lunch Cruise: $1 (that's not a misprint!)

Lunch cruises are a great innovation. At 12:15 every weekday, you can get on board the boat and take a half-hour cruise of Boston while eating your lunch. You can buy food onboard, but naturally I would suggest bringing your own.

EAST BOSTON FERRY

You've probably heard that you can take a water taxi to Logan Airport and that it costs a ridiculous $8. Well, here's some good news. As of recently, the MBTA runs a ferry out to East Boston from Long Wharf at the Marriott Long Wharf Hotel throughout the year, and it only costs $1. Trips run every 20 minutes during peak hours and at 10, 12 and 2 at midday. Once in East Boston, you can walk up the landing and then enter Maverick Square to get a real sense of the neighborhood. There are a couple of great restaurants to explore including Angelo's Pizzeria and La Famiglia (see the *Feasting Boston* chapter). For more details call the MBTA at 222-3200.

Other cruises and ferries (call for their cheapness):
    Boston Harbor Cruises 227-4321
    Massachusetts Bay Lines 740-4500
    Department of Environmental Management (Hingham to
        George's Island and between the harbor islands 740-1605
    A.C. Cruise Lines (Boston–Glouchester) 426-8419

AUCTIONS

I can name a couple of movies that have great romantic auction scenes. They may not be great movies, but they got one thing straight: auctions make for great dates. You're probably starting to feel a little threatened right now thinking how you couldn't possibly bid on any of those expensive items. Well, no one ever said you had to actually buy anything at the auction—we can save our money for the tag sales!

To find out when and where auctions are, check the *Boston Sunday Globe* (see Classified Index under "Auctions"). You may have to look hard to find the good ones, but they're there. Many of the auctions listed are the same day, while others are a few weeks in advance. If it doesn't say, call ahead to be certain that it is open to the public and that entry is *FREE*. (Sometimes they want you to buy an auction catalog, and these are not cheap!) Most listings will tell you the kind of stuff that will be on the block, and let you know if it is taking place at an auction house or at an estate.

Typically, you can stroll through the items on display before the live auction starts. This is a good chance for you and your date to talk about your likes and dislikes. Then, once the live auction begins, you can sit back and watch the bartering. It can be rather exciting at times, depending on what is being sold. Some auctions even serve refreshments for *FREE*.

MUSEUMS

Museums are some of the most impressive places to have dates. To those trained in the art of romancing, these rooms provide a plethora of amorous advantages. There is something about being surrounded by the greatest works of art that can turn any date into a memorable occasion and secure a repeat performance.

Museums should be a staple site for any real dater. Each room becomes a time machine transforming you and your companion into any time or place, be it early colonial American or Japanese temple. There is no question: art does inspire art, your art is dating!

Museums are also ideal for first or second dates, which can be intimidating. In a museum, there is little pressure to converse, as opposed to being in a restaurant where the only relief of the need to speak is the occasional, and often messy, mouthful. Yet these museums can spark a multitude of interesting conversations that will help you to get to know your companion better.

Tips for Museums:
1) Always call ahead. Hours of museums and libraries are nothing to guess at. They change often–*ESPECIALLY IN THE SUMMER*, as do the free hours. Call ahead to double check the hours and the *FREE* times. And remember many museums are *CLOSED ON MONDAYS*, so *ALWAYS CALL AHEAD*!

2) Plan ahead for eating. Most entries give a food suggestion, whether a nearby restaurant or advice to pack a picnic lunch to eat at the museum (see the *Eating Alternatives* section for picnic tips and ideas). If you do this, check your lunch with your coat and then retrieve it later.

3) Be sensitive to your companion's interests. Try to sense whether he or she is interested in the type of art presented at this museum. If not, don't take it personally; it is not a rejection of you, just of that particular subject matter. If this is the case, simply whip out *Cheap Dates* and suggest a different place and ask your date what he or she thinks.

ISABELLA STEWART GARDNER MUSEUM
    Every true romantic who has ever set foot in the Isabella Stewart Gardner Museum has had fantasies of wooing or being wooed within the beautiful courtyard of this Venetian-style palazzo. The lavishly decorated Gardner Museum is one of Boston's prize possessions. Mrs. Gardner built this museum when her private art collection

exceeded the limitations of her Beacon Street townhouse. "Mrs. Jack," as she was often called, lived on the fourth floor of the building, leaving the other three floors to house her art. The many floors of precious art wind around the center courtyard and skylight that illuminates the building like the heavens. Each room reveals Mrs. Gardner's impeccable taste, ingenuity of style and genius of acquisition. On your first visit, try the *FREE* Thursday tour. If you have never been to the Isabella Stewart Gardner Museum, this should be your next outing. And if you have been there, you will agree that it is worth visiting frequently. The MFA is around the corner from the Isabella Stewart Gardner Museum, so you can see both museums in one day, but this would probably risk sensory overload.

Another way to incorporate the Gardner Museum in your date without spending any money is to just visit the courtyard and ground floor. Admission is *FREE* to these parts of the museum. You and your companion can sit around the courtyard, peruse the gift shop, visit the current exhibit, or in summer go to the outdoor garden and cafe. This bottom floor is enough to impress any first-timer, and you can tempt your date with promises of two more floors on the next date.

Hopefully you'll be hungry when you go to the Isabella Stewart Gardner Museum, because they've got an excellent museum cafe with marvelous food for somewhat reasonable prices. The cafe has a fabulous new chef, Moncef, and serves soups, salads, panini and even gelato—all with an Italian influence. Mrs. Gardner's preference for things Italian didn't stop with artwork. During the warmer months, there is outdoor seating in her garden. You can also bring your own picnic lunch to eat outdoors—unfortunately the courtyard is off limits for snacks. If you want less glamour and lower prices, jump next door to Simmons College. They have a good cafeteria with even better prices. Go in the main entrance, take a right down the corridor and down the first flight of steps.

Also, don't pass up an opportunity to hear one of the Gardner's fantastic concerts. See the *Classical Music* section for details about this unmatched concert series.

ADDRESS 280 The Fenway, Boston.

PHONE 566-1401. For concert information call 734-1359.

PRICES Adults $7; Students $5; children under twelve *FREE*. Students pay $3 all day Wednesday. Always *FREE* for museum shop, cafe, and first floor.

HOURS Tue-Sun 11-5. *CLOSED MONDAYS*. Cafe Hours: Tue-Fri 11:30-3; Sat & Sun open until 4.

DIRECTIONS Located on the curvy Fenway Street that follows the Fens, the Isabella Stewart Gardner Museum is between Simmons College and the MFA, with a grassy park directly next door.

By T: Take the Green Line E train to the Ruggles/Museum stop. Take Museum Road past the MFA toward the green of the Fens. Bear left and it's on the corner of Fenway Street and Evans Way.

PARKING Meter parking normally isn't too difficult on the side streets surrounding the Isabella Stewart Gardner Museum. But if you are patient, you may even find an unmetered spot on curbs surrounding the grassy park next door. Otherwise, there is pay parking close by at the MFA.

MUSEUM OF FINE ARTS

If variety is something you desire in your dating life, then the MFA is for you. The overwhelming collection abounds in Asian, American, European, and even Modern art.

There is something for everyone here . . . even kids. Members are sent a seasonal publication of all the hundreds of activities, but anyone can pick up a free publication when you're there. If you plan to make the MFA a large part of your dating routine, then it may be worth it for you to become a member. For $50 a year, you and a guest will be admitted *FREE*, and get special privileges for major exhibits and discounts all over the museum (gift shop, films, lectures and parking). Even if you and a date go there five times a year, it'll be a saving. The calendar is filled with endless possibilities of concerts, lectures and films. See *Films* section for more information on the MFA's movies.

Another bonus at the MFA is that students from most of Boston's universities get in *FREE* with ID. These schools include: Art Institute of Boston, Berklee, BC, BU, Brandeis, Curry, Emerson, Emmanuel, Gordon, Harvard, Mass. College of Art, MIT, Montserrat, MFA School, NE School of Art and Design, Newbury College, Northeastern, Pine Manor, Roxbury Community College, Showa, Tufts, UNH, U-Mass-Boston, Wellesley, Wentworth, Wheaton and Wheelock. Considered as members, students of these schools also get 10 percent off of items from the gift shop; don't ever forget your student ID if you have one.

If you really want to dazzle your date or bone up on your art history, go on a *FREE* guided walk through the museum provided each day by the Ladies Committee. The walks are given Tuesday–Friday (sometimes on Saturdays), and last about an hour. Since the times always change, it is necessary to call or check the Information Center. Another terrific way to impress your date or to just treat yourself right is to go to the afternoon teas, also provided by the Ladies Committee. It's ridiculous to think that for $2 you get tea, cookies and live music with the amorous ambiance of the MFA. Teas are held Tuesday–Friday from 2:30 to 4:00; it's worth it to plan your visit around the teas.

There are several choices for food: You can go to the rather pricey restaurant on the first floor. You can eat light and well priced at Galleria which, with its sidewalk cafe ambiance in the center of things, is also a great place for people watching. You could have tea and a delicious pastry for about $10 for two. There is your average cafeteria food in the basement (pre-made sandwiches, fruit, yogurt and a few hot dishes), or you can bring your own picnic lunch to be eaten in the cafeteria, the adjacent courtyard, or the grounds surrounding the museum. If none of these on-the-premises options grabs you, then you can hop over to Simmons College for a variation on the cafeteria food (better priced and more variety). Simmons is next to the Isabella Stewart Gardner Museum on Fenway Street, about three blocks from the MFA.

ADDRESS 465 Huntington Avenue, Boston.

PHONE 267-9300 (recording of events), 267-2973 (recording of ticket info.)

PRICES $8 adults; $3.50 children 6-17; $5 seniors and students; *FREE* to members and students from most Boston area colleges (with ID). *FREE* to all on Wednesdays from 4 to 10.

HOURS Tuesday-Saturday, 10-4:45; Wednesdays 10-9:45; Sundays 10-5:45. The West Wing only (includes restaurants, auditorium, gift shop, and special exhibits) open Thursday and Friday until 9:45 p.m. CLOSED MONDAYS except on holidays.

DIRECTIONS The MFA is located on Huntington Avenue across from Northeastern University. Huntington Avenue is perpendicular to Mass. Ave. at Symphony Hall and the MFA is a half mile down Huntington Avenue toward Brookline.

By T: Take the Green Line E train to the Ruggles/Museum stop. The E line can only be taken from the Copley, Arlington, Boylston, Park Street and Government Center stops.

PARKING Meter parking surrounds the MFA on all sides (two-hour limit) or you can pay for parking at the Museum.

HARVARD UNIVERSITY MUSEUMS

Often lost amid Harvard University's glittering reputation for academic excellence are numerous hidden treasures. A fine university should not only offer an excellent education for its students, but it should benefit the community as well. Harvard has certainly fulfilled this requirement with the Harvard University Museums alone. If you have not yet taken advantage of the benefits of having Harvard across the river, the best place to start is at their museums.

THE HARVARD UNIVERSITY ART MUSEUMS

It is difficult to believe that one single institution, even one that has been around for so long, could acquire so many famous art works. But they did. Instead of throwing all of their pieces into one museum, the Harvard Art Museums have divided up their collection into three separate collections, each containing works from different regions of the world. Their smaller galleries will give you and your date the feeling of being in a small out-of-the-way Parisian gallery—except you'll be able to read the museum labels!

The Fogg

This is the most impressive of the three, featuring European and American art. No matter how unfamiliar you are with art, you'll be amazed at how many objects you recognize. If you only have time for one of the many museums, this should be it. A visit to the Fogg will whet your appetite and keep you coming back for more. The Fogg is also the largest of the art museums, and should take the most amount of time.

The Busch-Reisinger

Located above the Fogg is the Busch-Reisinger Museum featuring an interesting collection of Central and Northern European art. You may find that since most of the art is German (translated: extremely graphic and often morbid), it will spark many interesting conversations. The Busch-Reisinger is a tiny museum and should only take a few minutes to peruse.

The Sackler

The third museum in this great trio is the Sackler, located a half a block from the Fogg. The Sackler has a magnificent collection of Asian, Islamic and ancient art that really gives the MFA a run for its money.

For one low, low price (especially for students, so don't forget your college IDs), you get access to all three of these museums for the entire day. You can go to one museum, break for lunch in some chic Cambridge spot and then go back for more. Saturday mornings are the best time to go since the museum is *FREE* from 10 to 12. During these hours, they will give you pins and you can use them all day to get in and out of all three museums. Now that's a Cheap Date!

The Harvard Art Museums also provide *FREE*, more-than-decent docent tours once a day Tuesday through Friday in each of the museums. Learned volunteers will take you through the galleries and present you with an hour-long tour of the museum's finest and most interesting works. Each museum gives docent tours at different times, so you can get all three in one day: the Fogg at 11; the Sackler at 12; and the Busch-Reisinger at 2. Since hours change during the summer, call ahead to be certain.

While you are in the area, it will only heighten the experience to wander around Harvard Yard. Of course, the "Yard," as the Ivy Leaguers call it, is at its height during the autumn season. But regardless of when, Harvard has some beautiful buildings and spaces worth seeing. If the weather is nice, a picnic lunch in the Yard always provides the perfect ambiance (see the *Eating Alternatives* section for picnic tips). But if you want to get the real Harvard experience, go to Bartley's Burger Cottage nearby on Mass. Ave. Or, if you're in the mood for a chic, slightly alternative meal, go to Cafe Pamplona also nearby on Bow and Arrow streets. Both are cheap and can give some real insight into the life a Harvardite.

ADDRESS The Fogg and Reisinger: 32 Quincy Street, Harvard University. **The Sackler:** 485 Broadway at the corner of Quincy Street.

PHONE 495-9400.

PRICES $5 for adults; $3 for students and seniors; *FREE* for children under 18. *FREE* Saturdays 10–12!

HOURS Monday-Saturday 10–5; Sunday 1–5.

DIRECTIONS Quincy Street is perpendicular to Mass. Ave. (and Broadway at the opposite end) and runs along one side of Harvard Yard.

By T: Take the Red Line to the Harvard stop. From the exit, walk one block east to Quincy Street. Take Quincy Street almost to the end to the entrance of the Fogg (the Busch-Reisinger is reached through the Fogg). The Sackler is farther down Quincy Street at the corner of Broadway.

PARKING If you dare to drive, your best bet for parking is either the meter parking on Quincy Street across from the Fogg or other surrounding side streets away from Harvard Square.

HARVARD MUSEUMS OF NATURAL HISTORY

Despite having never been terribly interested in the scientific nature of things (pretty paintings have always been more appealing), I was utterly fascinated by the Harvard Museums of Natural History. I was also shocked at how romantic a museum of natural history could be. There is something about discovering all these artifacts of early man, and being surrounded by ferocious beasts and glorious gems, that makes the Harvard Museums of Natural History particularly romantic.

You'll be amazed at the amount of acquisitions that are "the oldest" or "the largest" or "rarest." Although there is tough competition, you'll find stranger life forms here than you will 300 yards away in Harvard Square. The Museum of Natural History consists of the Botanical Museum, the Mineralogical and Geological Museum, the Museum of Comparative Zoology, and the Peabody Museum of Archaeology and Ethnology, all under the same roof on the north side of Harvard Yard.

Admission is only $4 for adults ($3 for seniors and students, so bring your ID), and gives you access to all four museums, all day. All the museums can be hit in the same day, but to do so, a lunch or snack break is usually necessary. Make sure to keep the receipt they give you in order to come and go as you please. Just as the art museums have *FREE* admission one day a week, the Natural History Museums are *FREE* on Saturdays between 9 and 11. Call to make sure this hasn't changed!

The Botanical Museum

Your natural science discovery will expose you to all kinds of animals, vegetables and minerals from all ages (sound like an excursion into your refrigerator?), and then exhibit how we have come to learn this knowledge. You will begin this discovery at the Botanical Museum. If you have never seen the world-renowned "glass flowers," they probably won't be what you're expecting. Rather than an art exhibit of beautiful flowers akin to those of Renoir or Monet, this is a scientific endeavor that will amaze you with its realness. There are cross sections of roots, perfectly duplicated fruits, giant bees pollinating giant flowers and many other incredible accomplishments. Since there is no comparable collection elsewhere in the world, it is not advisable to bring a terribly clumsy date. You may do irreparable damage to the science of botany.

Museum of Comparative Biology

If you are squeamish about insects, tarantulas and other small pests, then you might want to skip the first room of the Museum of Comparative Zoology. Here you'll also find enough birds to keep you away from Hitchcock movies for life, underwater animal sounds that'll make you feel like Aquaman, and prehistoric monsters to make you thank God you were born in the 20th century. The two of you can shudder together at the awesome animals our earth has been home to. There are also hundreds of animals from every species imaginable. Even if science isn't your thing, you will undoubtedly be amazed at both the acquisitions of Harvard and what a strange world we live in. (Oh, if you were planning on wearing your alligator boots or the beaver coat, you may want to reconsider!)

Mineralogical and Geological Museum

For some couples, it may be dangerous to even enter the Mineralogical and Geological Museum. If your date has expensive tastes, you may never get out of there without promising jewels of all kinds.

Yes, they have fool's gold.

Here you'll see some of the largest gems and stones in existence. See what a real "diamond in the rough" looks like and explore the stages a gem goes through to become jewelry.

Peabody Museum of Archaeology and Ethnology

Now that you have seen the variety of animals, vegetables and minerals to which the world has been host, the Peabody Museum of Archaeology and Ethnology will show you how they were discovered and the different roles cultures play in the world. Everyone knows what archaeology is, but for those who aren't too familiar with ethnology, it is the study of different cultures, their folkways and customs. On view are giant totem poles, ancient games, representations of clothing styles, ground plans of excavations, North American Indian artifacts, cooking utensils and more. It is the oldest museum in the country devoted to archaeology and ethnology. Isn't it about time you got around to seeing it?

Make sure once you've seen all four museums that you check out Harvard's incredible museum shops. The larger one is at the front entrance of the museum. A smaller one is located at the back of the building near the Divinity Street exit. You should try to visit both since they have different items to offer. Undoubtedly, you will walk away with some great find.

When your feet become weary and you feel the need for rest coming on, the closest and quickest lunch spot is across the street at Bio Labs Cafe. It's your basic on-campus lunch spot with a spruced-up cafeteria style. Open Monday-Friday 7:30 to 5:00, the prices here are quite reasonable. The fare is wholesome with soups, chili, sandwiches and salads available every day. There are also special entrées available daily for $3-4. The dining area is clean and the clientele is brilliant! Try to listen in on some fascinating conversations. If you're visiting Harvard on a weekend when Bio Labs is closed, you either need to BYO lunch (plenty of good picnic opportunities) or venture into the Square.

Other Museums

While you're in the area (if you haven't had enough of science), you may want to check out two smaller museums nearby that Harvard has to offer. One is the Semitic Museum at 6 Divinity Street, which features some impressive finds from the Holy Land. The Semitic Museum is across Divinity Street from the Natural History Museum's back exit. Admission is usually *FREE*.

Another interesting, smaller museum is the Collection of Historical Scientific Instruments at 1 Oxford Street in the Science Center. From the front exit of the Natural History Museum, walk back down Oxford Street and enter the last building on the right. The collection is located on the lower level of the Science Center. A $5 admission is charged, but it's *FREE* on Saturdays, 9–11.

ADDRESS 11 Divinity Avenue, Harvard University.

PHONE 495-3045.

HOURS Mon-Sat 9-4:15; Sun 1-4:15.

PRICES Adults: $4; Students $3. *FREE* on Saturdays 9-11 (admission good for full day)!

DIRECTIONS From Harvard Square take Mass. Ave. north out of the Square and bear right onto Cambridge Street. Go under the underpass, take a left onto Quincy Street and another left onto Kirkland Street. From Kirkland Street take your first (and only) right onto Oxford Street. The Museum is about two blocks up on the right side of the street.

By T: Take Red Line to Harvard Square stop. Exit the station at the Harvard Hall exit and cross the Yard heading towards the Science

Center. Near the Science Center you will discover Oxford Street. Walk down Oxford Street to find the museum two blocks up the street on the right.

PARKING It is much easier to park around here than in the Square. Oxford Street usually has metered parking spots right out front of the museum. The meters are good for two hours, so bring quarters and be prepared to have to refill them at some time.

MUSEUM OF TRANSPORTATION AT LARZ ANDERSON PARK

The Museum of Transportation is another example of the unique museums Boston has to offer. This museum, built on the former estate of Larz Anderson in Brookline, is filled with the antiques he collected, and fine vintage cars. It is fascinating to see the style and manner in which Anderson lived and collected these beautiful cars. The museum also hosts contemporary car shows and auctions periodically. Call or stop by for more information about these.

Besides being a great museum to visit, it has beautiful grounds with intense picnic opportunities. If you are into photography, bring a camera; there are some neat old structures left over from the Andersons. From the peak of the property is an incredible view of Boston . . . a great place at sunset to sit in your car and neck. Larz Anderson also hosts outdoor ice skating in the winter. Call for more information.

ADDRESS 15 Newton Street, Brookline.

PHONE 522-6140.

PRICES $5 for adults; $3 for students.

HOURS Sat–Sun 10-5.

DIRECTIONS From Route 9 take Lee Street near the Brookline Reservoir. Follow Lee Street to the end and turn left onto Newton Street. Go right at the fork; the entrance is the next left.

PARKING Parking available on the premises.

INSTITUTE OF CONTEMPORARY ART (ICA)

Brace yourself for a truly contemporary experience. The ICA has no permanent collection and prides itself on exhibiting some of the world's most perplexing art in all mediums: painting, photography, sculpture, video and other media art. You may feel as if you just stepped into *A Clockwork Orange*, but give it time and before you know it, the art will begin to make a little sense (in a nonsensical kind of way). This is the interesting antithesis of the old Boston filled with tradition, propriety and etiquette; it can lead you to discover some of the city's hidden post-modern tendencies. The ICA is well equipped with a video room and plenty of programs for modern art lovers of all ages.

One thing to keep in mind is that the artwork here is a far cry from the sweet depictions of impressionism or the pious accomplishments from Middle Ages. In fact, some of the material shown here can be downright disturbing, so consider whether this is something that you and your date will be able to enjoy.

The hours at the ICA are as irregular as the art, so make sure you call first. The ICA shuts down while installing their next exhibit, so don't be surprised if they tell you they will be closed for two weeks. If you aren't too sure that you are going to love the ICA's array of art, then you are better off to try it during some of their free hours.

There is no place to eat in the ICA, but the neighborhood is filled with cuisine of all caliber. A yummy and cheap place to go during the day is the Pour House one block east of the ICA on Boylston Street. For fancier fare, Division 16, a former fire house next door to the ICA, is delicious with huge portions, but often prices to match. It is a good place to share an entrée or appetizer.

ADDRESS 955 Boylston Street, Boston.

PHONE 266-5152.

PRICES Adults $5.25; students $3.25. *FREE* to all Thur 5–9.

HOURS Wed–Sun 12–5; Thur 12–9; *CLOSED MONDAYS AND TUESDAYS. CALL, CALL, CALL BEFORE YOU GO!*

DIRECTIONS The ICA is located on Boylston Street near Mass. Ave. across from the Hynes Convention Center and next to Division 16.

By T: Take the Green Line to the Hynes Convention Center/Auditorium stop. From the exit walk toward Boylston Street and then one block east to the ICA.

PARKING Parking is difficult, but be patient and try the meter parking on some side streets or down Mass. Ave. by the Christian Science Church. Bring quarters!

THE COMPUTER MUSEUM

I hate computers. Ever since my little brother accidentally deleted my college admissions essay on my father's IBM, I have hated these things. So why would a person like me (and maybe you, too) ever want to set foot in a computer museum?

Because it is really cheap therapy.

Not only do you get to see one of the most unusual and amazingly fascinating museums, but you get to go inside a gigantic two-story computer to see what makes it tick, and beep, and stall and lose important documents . . . Anyway, it doesn't matter if you're DOS, Apple, Unix or Starbase literate or even if you're illiterate, this museum will fascinate the pants off you.

The Computer Museum will show you all the things we can do with computers these days: play Virtual Reality games, compose songs, draw elaborate scenes and make commercials—oh yeah, then there's some stuff about the computer's ability to solve the world's problems. Did I mention you can create cartoons? There is an Animation Theater and a newly enhanced Smart Machines Gallery that shows off a bunch of brilliant robots and some cool programs. You can take anyone, young or old, but the Computer Museum is especially fun for dates. You'll find an outing here will make you and your companion interactive, software compatible and user friendly.

All those computers can make you pretty hungry. If you're visiting the computer museum in the warmer months, you can try some of the yummy food at the Milk Bottle lunch stand located in the giant milk bottle (I'm guessing that's where they got the name). If seafood is your craving, you're in luck because the Barking Crab, that used to only be open summers, has just gone full time. Located in the warehouse at 88 Sleeper Street (at the corner of Northern Avenue), surrounded by blue lights, it is a beacon for seafood lovers. The ambiance is low maintenance, with picnic benches, paper plates and sand pails holding silverware. If you are here in the summertime, you can take this opportunity to get a look at some of the harbor islands. See *Harbor Cruises* section.

ADDRESS 300 Congress Street (Museum Wharf), Boston.

PHONE 423-6758 (computer info) or 426-2800 (somewhat human).

HOURS Tues–Sun 10–5 (hours vary in summer—call ahead). *CLOSED MONDAYS*, except Boston school holidays and vacations.

PRICES Adults $7; students and seniors $5; free for children under 4. *HALF PRICE ON SUNDAYS* 3–5 (call to verify).

DIRECTIONS The Computer Museum is located at Museum Wharf next to the huge milk bottle on Congress Street, off Atlantic Avenue.

By T: Take the Red Line to South Station and follow signs to the Museum Wharf.

PARKING Parking is difficult in this area. Your only hope is to try to find one of the few meter spots. Otherwise, be prepared to pay $2.50 per half hour.

NEW ENGLAND AQUARIUM

The New England Aquarium is truly romantic with its fascinating array of aquatic animals that dance and jump to entertain. But let's face it, the Aquarium has gotten too darn expensive. I've got some inherent gene that won't allow me to cross the threshold of a museum that costs more than I earn in an hour. Since the $8.75 admission fee falls into this category, the only time I can financially manage the Aquarium is on Terrific Thursdays. On Thursdays after 4 the Aquarium will take $1 off the admission. (Times and discounts change frequently so call ahead). And when you think of all the hours of unusual and incredible entertainment you get, it makes the people at the Aquarium seem very generous. In fact, it almost makes the $8.75 admission all right—but not quite. Then again, maybe you get paid more than I do, in which case the Aquarium might be within your budget.

If you really like the Aquarium, a membership would be smart. The Aquarium hosts tons of special exhibits and activities, even whale watches! So, go to the Aquarium, but try to go on Terrific Thursdays. If that's just not possible, then take the plunge and go anytime . . . just make sure not to call it a Cheap Date. If you want to save money in other areas, try one of the cheaper restaurants in the North End like La Famiglia or La Piccola Venezia. See *Eating Out* section for details.

ADDRESS Central Wharf, Boston.

PHONE 973-5200.

PRICES Adults $8.75; Seniors $7.75; Children (3-11) $4.75. Terrific Thursdays $1 off admission after 4 p.m.

HOURS Winter (Labor Day–June 30): Mon–Wed 9–5; Thur 9–8; Fri 9–5; Sat, Sun, Holidays 9–6. Summer hours: Mon, Tue, Fri 9–6; Wed, Thur 9–8; Sun, Sat, holidays 9–7.

DIRECTIONS Three blocks from Faneuil Hall Marketplace toward the water on the Freedom Trail. Follow the Aquarium fish signs. If driving north, take the Southeast Expressway Route 3 to

Atlantic Avenue exit. If driving south, exit at the Callahan Tunnel ramp and follow the signs.

By T: Take the Blue Line to Aquarium station. This is you best bet.

PARKING The Aquarium offers discount parking at a few of the local garages, including Rowes Wharf Hotel and the Garage at Post Office Square. Validate parking tickets at information booth at Aquarium.

LONGYEAR MUSEUM

It was such a pleasant surprise to stumble upon the Longyear Museum. One day I was driving around with a friend checking out all the magnificent homes in a posh Brookline neighborhood, wishing that I could take a peek in just one. Then suddenly there was this Victorian mansion at the top of a hill with a beautifully manicured lawn and a welcoming sign, "Longyear Museum and Historical Society: Home of Mary Baker Eddy." At the time I wasn't sure who this Mary Baker Eddy lady was, but I already knew I liked her style. She turned out to be the reason behind one of my other favorite Boston Beauties, The Christian Science Mother Church. Mrs. Eddy was the founder of Christian Science, and a couple of her homes are devoted to the teachings of her church.

But even if you don't have a whit of interest in the Christian Science religion, there is no denying that this museum is breathtaking and worth the visit. The hosts are extraordinarily welcoming and will answer all of your questions thoughtfully. There is also a lovely tour that will take you all around the house.

You can even pack a picnic and find a sweet spot on the grounds for lunch. Personally, I like to pretend that the mansion is mine and the butler is just waiting around the corner to obey my commands. You don't have to spend the whole day there, just make a nice outing of it when the weather is nice and you want to take a pretty drive around Brookline.

ADDRESS 120 Seaver Street, Brookline.

PHONE 277-8943.

HOURS Tue–Sat 10-4:15; Sun 1–4:15.

PRICES $3.

DIRECTIONS From Route 9 at the Brookline Reservoir, take a right at Chestnut Hill Avenue, then the next right and follow the signs to the museum.

PARKING Parking is available on the premises

PHOTOGRAPHIC RESOURCE CENTER (PRC) AT BOSTON UNIVERSITY

From the moment that you spot the PRC's funky glass doorway, it is apparent that this gallery caters to a more contemporary crowd. The PRC consists of three different galleries that normally exhibit three different shows filled with some impressive photographs. Exhibits running monthly and are usually filled with photography's latest issues, including AIDS, experimental art, feminism and hundreds of other topics from around the world. The gallery also boasts one of the city's best photography libraries. But if you're interested in a book, bring a pen and notebook to take notes, since this is a non-circulating library and they won't allow books off the premises.

Admission is cheap enough to make this one of your regular dating quarters. Since exhibits change monthly, you should go there at least that often so as not to miss anyof their scintillating shows.

ADDRESS 602 Commonwealth Avenue, Boston.

PHONE 353-0700.

HOURS Tues-Sun 12-5 and Thur until 8.

PRICES $3 for adults; $2 for students and seniors.

DIRECTIONS The PRC's front door is simple to find, right off Commonwealth Avenue at BU on Cummington Street, next to BU's School of Engineering.

By T: This is the easiest way to get to the PRC. Their door is 30 steps away from the Green B lines Blandford stop (first above-ground stop after Kenmore Square).

PARKING Meter parking is available all over the area, but can be tricky with all the BU students. The T stops right outside the PRC and is the best choice.

Just a couple more museums to see:
> **BOSTON TEA PARTY SHIP AND MUSEUM** Congress Street Bridge, Waterfront 338-1773.
> **COMMONWEALTH MUSEUM** 270 Morrissey Blvd., Dorchester 727-9268.

LIBRARIEʃ

The libraries in this chapter, for the most part, are historic institutions that are not only for the borrowing of books. They also hold the more valuable treasures of Boston's past, including the city's oldest volumes, prints, photographs, records and archives. Whether you're in search of the perfect volume, or simply taking in the serenity of the surroundings, these few spots are sure to be everything you could want in a romantic hideaway.

But the greatest part about libraries is the cost . . . nothing! Here in the Hub all of the libraries are *FREE*. What more could you want on a date? Interesting objects, romantic environs, and no admission charged!

THE BOSTON ATHENAEUM

It's very surprising to find that the Boston Athenaeum is such a well kept secret in Boston. Every visit to the intensely beautiful rooms of the Athenaeum speaks volumes about the private life and history of Boston and its people. Founded in 1807, the Athenaeum is one of the nation's oldest independent libraries and was the original home of many of the art works now at the MFA. Today, it continues to be a leading research facility for rare volumes, prints, historical source materials and archives dating back to the Civil War and Colonial days.

If this kind of stuff is interesting to you, then you would benefit greatly from a membership. You will always have a quiet oasis from hectic city life, get invited to some excellent social functions, be able to borrow books from their extensive stacks and get to enjoy their scrumptious weekly teas. In total, a $50 per year membership in the Athenaeum will greatly enrich your life.

But, what if a membership isn't in your future? Well, you can still partake in the rich ambiance of the Athenaeum by taking one of the Tuesday or Thursday tours. The tour is *FREE*, but you need to make a reservation the day before you go (if there are no reservations, they will not plan a tour). Usually beginning at 3, the 45-minute tour will give you a view of the entire breathtaking building. You'll find the reading rooms in the upper stories particularly beautiful with semi-private hideaways here and there, and the great views overlooking the Granary Cemetery especially marvelous in spring and summer.

If you don't know anything about the Athenaeum, you owe it to yourself to take one of these tours. Chances are that after this, you'll be ready to visit the Membership Office to see about becoming a member. While you're in the area, a trip to the Brattle Book Shop on West Street will only enhance your date. Browse through the "books for buck" tables and exchange gifts with each other.

ADDRESS 10-1/2 Beacon Street, Boston.

PHONE 227-0270.

HOURS Mon–Fri 9–5; some Saturdays 9–3:30. Only open to the public (other than a quick peek at the first floor) Tuesday and Thursday; tours at 3. Call ahead to make reservations.

PRICES *FREE*

DIRECTIONS The Athenaeum is just down Beacon Street from the State House in the direction of Faneuil Hall and downtown.

By T: Exit at Park Street station. Walk up Park Street towards the golden dome of the State House and then take a right onto Beacon Street until you get to the red doors of the Athenaeum.

PARKING If you try to drive to the Athenaeum, you are a braver soul than I. Parking is difficult in this area, but at least the Boston Common parking lot has been reopened with its entrance on Charles Street.

BOSTON PUBLIC LIBRARIES

MAIN BRANCH AT COPLEY SQUARE

Now that the Boston Public Library's (BPL) main entrance on Dartmouth Street has finally been restored, you've a better reason than ever to make this not-so-hidden treasures part of your dating ritual.

What's so great about a library for a date? you ask.

You'll see.

To start your acquaintance with the BPL, take their daily "Art and Architecture" tour. This is a great Boston freebie. You will be given a semi-private one-hour tour—although most tour guides could spend hours with you detailing the rich history of the library. The tour takes you through the lavishly detailed McKim Building, which is filled with so many rare and beautiful art pieces that it should be considered a museum. The McKim building holds impressive permanent exhibits, as well as some truly interesting temporary ones.

But the *pièce de résistance* — the place where every date should be whisked away to — is the courtyard. The open courtyard is the perfect place to steal away from a busy day or plan a secret rendez-vous. Bring a packed lunch and eat outdoors in a spot that will convince you that you've been transported to Italy. Even during the cold winter months, the courtyard is worth a visit.

Other than the gorgeous McKim building, the BPL's main branch provides many films, lectures and other events that can be a treat any night of the week. Check local newspaper listings for the weekly lineup (see *Film* section). If the main branch in Copley Square is a bit out of your way, check your local branch and find out what kind of activities they host.

ADDRESS 666 Boylston Street, Copley Square.

PHONE 536-5400.

HOURS Mon–Fri 9–9; Sat 9–5; *CLOSED SUNDAYS.*

PRICES *FREE*

DIRECTIONS The BPL is the enormous building on Boylston Street between Dartmouth and Exeter streets on Copley Square.

By T: The T is the smartest way to the BPL because the Copley station on the Green Line is directly below the BPL.

PARKING Parking is difficult on Boylston Street, but there are often spaces behind the library and on the side streets. Remember, this is all meter parking (usually two-hour limit) and they ticket like hounds.

NEWTON BRANCH

All of the BPL branches are good, but one of the newest is particularly impressive. If you ever find yourself in Newton, you have to check out their new and improved Newton Free Library. They have a fantastic collection of books, plus activities, exhibits, lectures and films galore. It is a wonderful place to hang out on a rainy day without spending a dime. There are listening rooms, new book rooms, periodicals from all over, books on tape, CDs, videos, comfortable chairs and great desks straight out of the Library of Congress. Wednesdays are *FREE* movie nights, and the other days of the week are also filled with events for every age. You can pick up the current newsletter anytime you're there, or you can get on the mailing list by becoming a Friend of the Newton Free Library for $10 a year. But the best deal is that as long as you have a BPL card, you can borrow from this library too.

While you're in the area, it is hard to miss the sprawling lawns of Newton Town Hall across the street. Go for a walk inside this beautiful building, or have a picnic lunch next to their rippling creek.

ADDRESS 330 Homer Street, Newton.

PHONE 552-7145.

HOURS Mon–Thur 10–9; Fri 10–6; Sat 9–5; Sun 1–4.

PRICES *FREE*

DIRECTIONS From Commonwealth Avenue going west in Newton, take a left onto Walnut Street at the Town Hall and then your first right turn onto Homer Street. The library is on your left.

By T: Take the Green Line D train to the Newton Highlands stop. From there (Walnut Street) either walk 1-1/2 miles north on Walnut Street to Homer Street, or catch the 59 Bus to City Hall at Walnut and Homer streets.

PARKING The Newton Free Library has free parking on the premises.

WIDENER LIBRARY

You can hardly be a Bostonian without having at least heard about the Widener Library at Harvard University. It is, after all, the third-largest library in the US and the largest university library in the world. But, honestly, so what if it's real big, its gotta have something cool to offer. Right? How about 12 million volumes, one of the few copies of the Gutenberg Bible, a first folio of Shakespeare, gorgeous stained-glass windows, and tons of *fine* fine art. Mr. Harry Widener's great misfortune was taking an untimely trip on the *Titanic*. He never returned to Boston, but had bequeathed money and books to the university and his mother saw to it that the Widener Library was built in his honor. In addition to over seeing this undertaking, Mrs. Widener, being convinced that Harry would've survived the disaster had he been able to swim, made a stipulation that every Harvard student must pass a swimming test to graduate from the university. Just one of the many interesting quirks about Harvard!

Tours of the library are particularly beneficial to give you a general sense of the greatness of this institution. To set up a tour, contact a reference librarian, either by phone or in person. The Widener collection room (where the Gutenberg Bible and many of the other great treasures of the library are) is one of the few parts of the library that is open to the public, but unfortunately it is not always open when the library is open. Hours are very erratic, so call ahead to be certain that there will be someone there.

Don't forget to pack a picnic lunch to have in Harvard Yard. If you are really liking the Harvard experience, then try a *FREE* Harvard University walking tour. Go to the Holyoke Information Center next door to Au Bon Pain (you know, the place where people play chess all day long) and ask when the next tour is being given.

ADDRESS 1329 Mass. Ave., Harvard University, Cambridge.

PHONE 495-2411.

PRICES *FREE*.

HOURS Widener collection room is normally open 9:30–10:30; 11:15–2:45; 3:15–4:30. But call ahead to be certain.

DIRECTIONS The Widener is located on Mass. Ave. in the heart of Harvard Square with another entrance in Harvard Yard.

By T: The T is the best way to get there. Take the Red Line to

Harvard station. From exit cross Mass. Ave. and walk down it toward Central Square to find the Widener on your left side.

PARKING Unfortunately, the old adage isn't true: you can't pahk yah cah in Hahvahd Yahd. But you can try along Mass. Ave. or Quincy Street.

OUTDOOR ACTIVITIES

One great thing about Boston is that each season of the year offers a whole different genre of outdoor activities that make for great dates.

Charles River Boat Company, Science Park, Boston 742-4282.

Pedal your own boat around the Charles River Basin for 40 minutes, leaving from Science Park near the Galleria Mall. The cost is only $6.

Swan Boats, Public Garden, Boston 522-1966.

If you're feeling lazy, let someone else man-power the boat (also makes for a great summer job if you want to stay in shape). Tours around the little pond at the Public Garden last about 15 minutes and only cost $1.75 ($.50 for children). Don't forget a picnic lunch for afterwards.

Community Boating House, Charles River Esplanade, Boston 523-1038.

Maybe you and your date would like to learn how to sail this summer. Memberships are very reasonable ($80 per month—better discounts for longer periods of time) and include the use of the boathouse, boats, equipment and even instructions. Or you can learn on your own and then really impress a date by taking him or her out for a spin!

Arnold Arboretum, 251 The Arborway, Jamaica Plain 524-1717.

Just a piece of Frederick Law Olmsted's emerald necklace, the Arboretum is open every day from dawn to dusk. There is tons to see and learn. At the visitors center there is a gift shop, videos about the Arboretum and listings for lectures and workshops. Call for details.

Franklin Park Zoo, Blue Hill Avenue, Dorchester 442-2002.

This newly revitalized zoo has much to offer for kids and adults alike. Admission is only $5 ($2.50 for kids) and will entertain you for the whole day.

Charles River Canoe Center, 2401 Commonwealth Avenue, Newton 965-5110.

For only $7 an hour you and your date can paddle all the way to Boston Harbor if you dare. There are plenty of places to stop for picnics—just remember to bring your bug spray, sunscreen and a great lunch.

Concord Canoe Service, Concord, 508-369-9438.

A great chance to canoe past some of the monuments of Lexington and Concord. Take a picnic lunch. Stop under a spreading tree along the shore. Enjoy.

Boston Harbor Sailing Club, 72 East India Row, Boston 523-2619.

Boston Sailing Center, 54 Lewis Wharf, Boston, 227-4198.

Boston Public Sailing, Piers Park, 95 Marginal Street, East Boston, 567-6400.

This is the *real* bargain among all the sailing operations in the Boston area. It is part of Massport and is a wonderful component of the East Boston redevelopment program along Boston Harbor.

Jamaica Pond Boathouse, 507 The Jamaica Way, Jamaica Plain 522-6258.

Weston Ski Track, 200 Park Road, Weston 891-6575.

Wonderful cross country skiing for about $10 per day. They also rent skis (about $9), have instructions, make snow, and even have night skiing. It's a wonderful, romantic getaway without going too far from home.

MDC Ice Skating Various locations, 727-9548.

The Metropolitan District Commission (MDC) has many ice skating facilities throughout Boston. Call your local branch or the main number above to find out where and when. The skating season usually lasts from mid-November to mid-March. Skating sessions normally only cost about $5.

Larz Anderson Skating Rink, 12 Newton Street, Brookline 730-2081. (Brookline Parks Department).

Skating at this beautiful outdoor skating rink on the old foundation of the Anderson estate will certainly take you back in time. Sessions vary from year to year, so call the Brookline Parks Department for details. They also rent skates. Don't forget your muffler!

BEYOND BOSTON

One of the many benefits of living in Boston is being able to leave it to discover the beauty of New England without too much hassle. Having a car is very helpful for most of these entries. If you don't have a car, simply contact the MBTA hotline at 722-3200, tell them where you want to go and they will give you all the information for taking public transportation. When planning your outing, remember to take appropriate clothes (it usually gets a little cooler outside of Boston), a picnic lunch to cut your eating costs, perhaps a book of poetry, a bottle of wine (and a corkscrew), a sketch book and whatever else will make your trip perfect.

The area around Boston has hundreds of beautiful spots, and the entries below represent only a small fraction of these. There are a couple of good books written about out-of-Boston excursions (not to be confused with out-of-body excursions), which can be found at your local bookstore. Start your exploration of Boston's environs with these few entries, and soon you'll find yourself packing up to escape the summer city heat, view the beautiful fall foliage, do some snow hiking or take in the glorious spring blossoms.

BEAUPORT

Beauport is the name that was given to Gloucester Harbor by Samuel de Champlain in 1606, and then taken for Henry Davis Sleeper's gorgeous mansion built overlooking the harbor facing west. A one-hour guided tour lets you peek at 25 of the 40 rooms of the Sleeper-McCann summer home. In 1907, Mr. Sleeper, a well-known Boston architect and interior designer, began a 26-room house using paneling from an 18th-century farmhouse. Gradually, over the next three decades, Mr. Sleeper expanded Beauport room-by-room to the present palatial 40-room estate. Each room has been decorated to represent a different period of American history. Take the tour, stroll the grounds, propose marriage—whatever you feel like. No matter what, it's a gorgeous sight!

ADDRESS 75 Eastern Point Boulevard, Gloucester.

PHONE 508-283-0800.

HOURS Open from mid-May to mid-October, Mon-Fri 10–4; Open on weekends mid-September to mid-October 1–4.

PRICES $4.

DIRECTIONS Take Route 128 North to the end; follow the sign for East Gloucester and follow for one and a half miles to Eastern Point Boulevard. Follow this for half a mile to Beauport.

By MBTA: From North Station, take the Rockport commuter train to Gloucester. From there, take a cab to Beauport for just a couple of dollars or walk following the above directions. It's a long but pretty walk, and you can see all the beautiful houses on the way.

HAMMOND CASTLE

It's funny to think that John Hayes Hammond, Jr. was a great inventor of radio control and guidance, television and high-speed communications, yet probably his greatest gift to mankind is this wonderful castle high on a cliff above Gloucester Harbor looking across at Beauport. Mr. Hammond was also a great traveler, and brought back stained-glass windows, furniture, arms and armor, floor tiles, doorways, facades, and whole buildings, the more Medieval the better. Seeing as he had brought over all this junk from Europe, he had to have someplace to put it all, so he built Hammond Castle. The castle is decorated in a myriad of periods (but mostly revolves around a grandiose Medieval style), and includes many oddities like the enormous 8,200-pipe organ—the largest ever built in a private home. The most spectacular (or at least one of them) is the glass-roofed pool solarium. It's a 30,000-gallon pool that can be filled with either salt or fresh water, and is surrounded by Roman ruins and Medieval pieces. It's incredible!

Guided tours are entertaining and extremely informative, helping to interpret this wonderful collection of Roman, Medieval and Renaissance art, explain how certain accoutrements were used in their day, and even display some of Mr. Hammond's inventions—he was, after all, second only to Thomas Edison. The castle is also host to many special organ concerts, haunted Halloween nights, murder mysteries and Christmas celebrations. It can be rented out for special events—but before you set your sights on getting married or even throwing a big bash here, be warned that it's probably out of your Cheap Date budget. However, you can enjoy a nice picnic on the grounds, provided you dispose of your trash appropriately and don't pick the flowers. There are some great vistas, so don't forget your binoculars!

ADDRESS 80 Hesperus Avenue, Gloucester.

PHONE 508-283-7673.

HOURS Open mid-May to mid-September, Mon–Fri 10–4. Mid-September to mid-May open only on weekends 10–4.

PRICES Adults $6; Students and seniors $5; children $4.

DIRECTIONS From Route 128 North, take exit 14, Route 133 to Gloucester; turn right at the beach onto Route 127, go up the hill and turn left onto Hesperus Avenue

By MBTA: From North Station, take the Rockport commuter train to Gloucester. From there take a cab to Hammond Castle.

PEABODY ESSEX MUSEUM, SALEM

The oldest continuously operating museum in the United States, the Peabody Essex Museum was founded when Salem's merchant captains had collected so many odds and ends from all over the world that they needed someplace to put it all. The museum is filled with natural wonders and man-made curiosities that will tickle your fancy to no end. Although there are halls of Chinese export porcelain, extraordinary Oriental furniture, and contents of Tokyo tradesmen's shops from the mid-1800s, the flavor is still maritime and ethnographic. You'll see the finest examples of ship models; marine paintings; scrimshaw and ivory work done by sailors; charts and navigation instruments, ancient and modern; a dory with all its Grand Banks cod fishing gear; a full range of equipment from the South Seas Whale Fishery; costumes, weapons, drums and temples of the Pacific islanders; and a whole gallery devoted to steam navigation. A favorite spot for many visitors is the great hall on the second floor of the original building, with its high ceilings, wavy glass and ships' figureheads ranged around the walls.

There is much much more for you to enjoy at the Peabody Essex Museum, but I'll leave it for you and your date to discover. There is a fantastic gift shop, and if you want to take a break from your viewing, there are a number of eateries along the Essex mall—the Peabody Essex Museum is one of those wonderful museums that let you come and go all day long for one price.

While you're in Salem, you can walk by the House of Seven Gables, but don't pay the $7 to get in—you'll get just as much from a free viewing from outdoors. If you have a car, drive down Derby Street (you can see Pickering Wharf and the old Customs House on the way) about a mile and half to Salem Willows Amusement Park. There is ample parking there, shady trees, beaches, hotdog stands, games, pinball machines and rowboats for hire—a Cheap Daters, dream come true!

ADDRESS East India Square, Salem, MA

PHONE 508-745-1876. Taped info: 508-745-9500.

HOURS Tue–Sat 10–5; Sun 12–5. CLOSED MONDAYS.

PRICES Adults $7; Students and seniors $6; Children $4; and a family rate of $18—so bring your parents and really make it a bargain!

DIRECTIONS Take Route 128 to exit 26, Lowell Street, Peabody. Go through Peabody Center 2.4 miles, turn left after Dunkin' Donuts onto Bridge Street, (Route 107). Go 1.2 miles to Winter Street (1-A), and turn right. Follow 1-A past Salem Common and left onto Essex Street near Hawthorne Hotel. Take a right onto Essex Street and then a right or left into a parking lot.

By MBTA: From North Station take the Rockport/Ipswich Line to Salem. From the Salem Depot the museum is nearby. Ask someone for directions.

PARKING Municipal parking is available for about $1 an hour.

CRANE BEACH

There are plenty of beaches closer to the city, but none really compare to Crane Beach—any time of the year. The parking costs are pretty steep, though cheaper during the off season, but it's still worth it for all the endless dunes, nature walking, tidal estuaries, marshy grass, rocky headlands and breathtaking views. In other words, for just a couple of bucks you getta whole lotta great makeout spots! In summer, the beach is well populated, making it fun for a group or to meet others. In fall and winter it's fun to bundle up and take some really nice walks along the shore. There are seasonal food stands by the parking lot, but since we are Cheap Daters, this beach screams out for the biggest, bestest picnic lunch you can haul along. Don't forget to bring: a blanket, binoculars, a camera, sunscreen (any season), bug spray, reading material, some good grub (at certain times of the year you can even stop at roadside vendors for fresh foods) and maybe even some watercolors. It's a blast!

On your way home, consider stopping at Woodman's in Essex for a bowl of the Bay State's best clam chowda! At the very least, stop at Goodale Orchard to pick your own something or other.

ADDRESS Crane Beach, Ipswich.

HOURS Open dusk until dawn all year round.

PRICES Parking costs vary depending on the season, but can be upwards of $8 per car.

DIRECTIONS From Route 128 North, take exit 15 and turn left at the foot of the off-ramp towards Essex. Turn left in Essex onto Junction 133, follow about four miles, to signs for Ipswich, then Castle Hill/Crane Beach. After you pass the Goodale Orchard sign, you have about two more miles to go.

CONCORD/LEXINGTON

There are numerous historical houses, fields, bridges and museums to visit in both these towns. Together they make a fun-filled day trip or even two days.

Once you've entered the center of Concord, you will probably start seeing all sorts of National Parks Services signs to guide you on your journey. You may want to start at the North Bridge Visitor Center (follow signs from Concord Center) to orient yourself. But first you will cross the Concord Bridge, which is the site of "the shot heard round the world." This is a particularly romantic spot. Then on to the Visitors Center to gain a historical background from their wide variety of exhibits—all of which is *FREE*. There is also a nice little bookstore to browse in and pick up a pamphlet or two to help guide your visit. The woods and area surround is extremely bucolic and perfect for a romantic walk.

ADDRESS North Bridge Visitors Center: 171 Liberty Street, Concord.

PHONE 508-369-6993.

HOURS Open year round 9:30–4 (open later in summer).

PRICES AND PARKING *FREE*

THE OLD MANSE

After a nice ramble over the extensive wooded park land on the far side of the bridge, you can come back past the Minuteman statue and the obelisk put up in 1836 and cross the field on your right to get to the Old Manse. The Old Manse is the house built in 1769–1770 by Ralph Waldo Emerson's father, who worked on the land, cheered on the patriots and helped the wounded during the Battle of Concord Bridge. Nathaniel Hawthorne rented this house for a few years in the 1840s.

ADDRESS Monument Street, Concord.

PHONE 508-369-3909. Off season call Trustees of Reservations: 508-840-4446.

HOURS April to October open Mon–Sat 10–5; Sun 1–5.

PRICES Adults $5.

CONCORD MUSEUM

Some say that the Concord Museum is the best place to start your visit, but I think you can do it any time during your trip. Located a few blocks from Concord Center on Lexington Road, it has period rooms from three centuries of domestic life, including Emerson's study, collections from other authors like Thoreau and the Alcott's and frequent special exhibitions on local history. It's a good place to pick up detailed information on all the other historical attractions in the area.

ADDRESS 200 Lexington Road (Route 2A), Concord.

PHONE 508-369-9763.

HOURS Open year round Mon–Sat 9–5; Sun 12–5. Hours frequently change, so call ahead.

PRICES Adults $6; Students $3.

GREAT MEADOWS WILDLIFE REFUGE

In Concord Center there are signs to the Great Meadows Wildlife Refuge, which is only a few minutes to the north on Monsen Road. Here you will find a great many pretty trails, and it's *FREE*.

WALDEN POND

A little way out of the center on Route 126 is the famed Walden Pond, where you can swim, go boating or just walk the surrounding woods with your copy of Thoreaus' *Walden* to muse, and feel first hand the observations experienced by the author over 100 years ago. Unfortunately, much of the serenity and peace no longer exist at Walden Pond, but a trip will fill you with renewed love of the land. Don't forget your swimsuit or your picnic!

ADDRESS Route 126, Concord.

PHONE 508-369-3254.

HOURS Open daily from 5 to a half hour after sunset. How romantic!

PRICES *FREE*, but only 1,000 people are allowed in the park at once. In summer, you may want to call ahead to see what your chances are.

PARKING There is parking for 350 cars.

In addition to these spots, there are plenty of other local sites that are worth your time. The **Orchard House** is the home of Louisa May Alcott, author of *Little Women*. Having read the book (or even seen the movie) guests will see exactly how her surroundings affected her novels. For more information call 369-4118. Near the Orchard House is the **Wayside**, a house owned by Samuel Whitney (I have no idea who he was), but was later inhabited by Nathaniel Hawthorne, the Alcotts and the Lothrops. Call 369-6875 for details, or ask around.

A fantastic topper to your day trip to Lexington and Concord is the **Nashoba Valley Winery** in Bolton. You can get a half-hour tour of the winery and see all the stages of wine making—you even get to taste the finished product. Mmm. Nashoba Valley Winery also has seasonal fruit picking, which turns any date into a memorable one. Make sure to call ahead to see what's ripe for the picking. It's a great place to take your picnic lunch or dinner, and you can even buy some of their wines to take home. Call 508-779-5521.

DE CORDOVA MUSEUM

Opened in June of 1996 newly renovated, the De Cordova in Lincoln is just beyond Route 128 and sits on a 35-acre sculpture park. This part of the museum is *FREE*, and worth the trip, even if you don't want to pay to get into the museum. Blanket picnicking is highly smiled upon.

The museum concentrates on showcasing the work of living New England artists—yet it still has some wonderful examples dating from before the 1940s. Much of the artwork featured is contemporary, in media of all kinds including paintings, graphic arts and photography.

ADDRESS 51 Sandy Pond Road, Lincoln.

PHONE 259-8355.

HOURS Tues–Fri 10–5. Sat–Sun noon–5.

PRICES Adults $4; Students $3

DIRECTIONS Take Route 2 west to Route 128 south. Get off at exit 28 west and drive three and a half miles to the museum.

By MBTA: From North Station take the Fitchburg commuter train to the Lincoln station. Ask directions from there. You can even rent bikes there and ride out to the museum.

PARKING Plenty of free parking available.

DRUMLIN FARMS

You may want to complement your visit with a trip to Drumlin Farms. Drumlin Farms is a large demonstration farm as well as the headquarters of the Massachusetts Audubon Society. Although it is mostly geared toward children, even daters benefit from seeing all the animals and seeing first-hand how a New England farm is run. Drumlin Farms also hosts many lectures, activities, clinics and other fun stuff for everyone. Call 259-9807 for more details.

GORE PLACE

Built in 1806 as a country mansion for Christopher Gore and his family, Gore Place is considered one of the finest examples of Federal architecture existing. The mansion sits on a beautiful 45 acres of landscaped grounds that are open to the public year round. An hour tour of the interior of the house will take you through a series of spacious and pleasing rooms, decorated with furniture, paintings, carpets, china and other lavish stuff from the early 19th century. There is an incredible spiral staircase in the formal entry that reaches up three full flights of the building.

The Gore family was at the forefront of early American agri-cultural reform, and to this day the estate is still a working farm. You can even meander the fields to find a small flock of sheep near the quaint farmer's cottage built in 1835. The grounds are perfect for a picnic, but please don't feed the sheep!

ADDRESS 52 Gore Street, Waltham.

PHONE 894-2798.

HOURS Open April 15 to November 15. Tues–Sat 10–5; Sun tours are given at 1, 2, 3 and 4 p.m.

PRICES Adults $4.

DIRECTIONS Take 128 to exit 26 towards Waltham onto Route 20. Follow Route 20, which is Main Street, to Gore Street and take a right to find the house on the left side.

By bus: Take the 70 Bus from Central Square. Walk to Gore Street and find the house on the left side.

PARKING Free parking available on premises.